ON THE JOURNEY

A MARRIED COUPLE'S STUDY GUIDE

DR. MAX W. REAMS

COMPANION BOOK:

BEFORE YOUR JOURNEY
A PREMARITAL STUDY GUIDE

Good marriages do not just happen. They must be nurtured and carefully maintained. Two key elements needed to develop and sustain a good marriage are communication and a shared spiritual life. With that in mind, Dr. Max Reams provides a rich set of devotionals that will help couples enrich their marriage relationship. These 60 daily devotionals are designed to assist couples as they cultivate the habit of sharing a daily devotional time. Dr. Reams' words are practical, biblical, and time-tested in his own marriage and in countless counseling sessions with young couples. These devotionals have wide appeal—they will be helpful to newlyweds and the "not-so-newlyweds" as well. I highly recommend *On the Journey*.

Dr. John C. Bowling, President, Olivet Nazarene University

We don't know of a professor who has had more impact over more years at Olivet than Dr. Max Reams. His five decades of teaching have not been limited to his classroom, however. All of us who are fortunate enough to know Max have benefited from the passion he and Carol share for ministering to couples on our campus and beyond. That's why this resource is so eagerly anticipated. Consider it your roadmap for an incredible journey of walking together with God. Packed with inspiration and biblical wisdom, this resource will help the two of you join your spirits like never before.

Drs. Les & Leslie Parrott, #1 New York Times bestselling authors of *Saving Your Marriage Before It Starts*

Each of the 60-day readings in *On the Journey* is brimming with relational wisdom and scriptural truth balanced with contemporary research and resources. The result will jumpstart your marital journey toward a healthy and joyous path. Here is a book you will treasure!

David J. Wine, Discipleship Pastor, GatheringPoint Church of the Nazarene and Associate Professor of Christian Ministry, Olivet Nazarene University

BACKGROUND

These devotionals are modified from thoughts shared in classes when I taught at Olivet Nazarene University. This book is a response to student requests that the thoughts become available in print. Additional material is drawn from retreats for married couples, led by my wife, Carol Reams, and me. This collection is not intended in any way to replace marital counseling or therapy. Nor are all topics related to marriage discussed. My hope is that this material may assist married couples' devotionals, prayer time, and discussions, and also encourage marital counseling with a trained counselor or pastor, if appropriate.

Scripture quotes are from the New International Version Bible (NIV)

Cover Photo: Courtesy of Joe Mantarian

Cover Design: Randall Rupert

DISCLAIMER

The information provided in this book is for inspirational purposes only. It is not intended or implied to be a substitute for professional marital advice, diagnosis, or treatment. Always consult with a marital counseling professional with any questions you may have prior to making a decision regarding the information based on what you have read in this book. Never disregard professional advice, or delay in seeking it, because of something you have read in this book or in the content of the links or references in the content resources. The author does not endorse nor necessarily agree with information in the linked resources or references.

ACKNOWLEDGMENTS

I am thankful to the staff of Olivet Nazarene University's Office of Institutional Advancement for their heartfelt support to help make this book possible. I am grateful to my editor, Laura Warfel, and to my thoughtful and insightful volunteer readers. Barbara Axmark provided insight regarding formatting. Randall Rupert gave important assistance with layout and other details. I appreciate everyone for their excellent suggestions and careful work. Their contributions have greatly improved the text. All errors are mine.

DEDICATION

This book is dedicated to Carol, my wife and chief encourager, without whom this book would never have seen the light of day, and to our children, grandchildren, and great-grandchildren.

HOW TO USE THIS BOOK

These 60 devotionals are designed to be read by couples after referring to the scripture references. Questions are provided to assist in discussion. Prayer points and take-aways are for further thought. The devotionals are arranged in a degree of order, but most can be read as stand-alone entities. Space is provided for notes and responses.

TABLE OF CONTENTS

WHAT ATTRACTS ONE PERSON TO ANOTHER?

Read: Song of Songs 1:15 and 1:16a

Focus: "How beautiful you are, my darling! Oh, how beautiful! Your eyes are doves." . . . "How handsome you are, my lover! Oh, how charming!"

Studies dealing with what initially attracts couples together usually list physical attraction as one of the beginning factors. There is no universal understanding of what is physically attracting for couples, since superficial appearance is only one possibility. Visual appearance is often just a prelude to discovering what the other person is like in a variety of ways. Sometimes the attraction has little to do with culturally perceived beauty or handsomeness.

As an outsider looking on, you may have wondered what attracted some couples you have known. Sometimes the attraction had little to do with what our culture defines as physical attractiveness. The magnet may have been aesthetic, such as between two people who share a common love for music or art. Others were attracted because they share a common goal, purpose, interest, or religious perspective. The possibilities are endless!

Attraction can occur between people who come from similar backgrounds. This explains why individuals who live near each other are often attracted together. Similar family patterns and expectations can also draw one person to another. It is no surprise that many individuals find themselves attracted to their fellow classmates in high school or college. Others meet in work settings that arise from common career pursuits. Those of similar cultural backgrounds, whether regional or local, may find comfortable connections. Shared religious experiences can be attractive, especially for committed believers.

Personality similarities or differences also play a role in some attractions. Feeling relaxed in the presence of another may be attractive, whether due to commonalities or unlike characteristics. Opposites often attract, but so do nearly identical personalities.

In order for a relationship to grow, however, much work needs to be done. The initial attraction is rarely adequate to sustain a significant connection for a couple. Our society often focuses on trivial characteristics, such as physical appearance and how good someone is in bed. As time goes on, such relationships often dry up, and a dull monotony sets in. Happy and growing couples have learned that there is much more to a good marriage than the superficiality fostered by the media.*

Resource:
The DNA of Relationships, Gary Smalley, Tyndale House Publishers.

Discussion Questions:
1. Describe attractions you felt for each other when you first met.

2. Describe specific attractions you feel for each other now.

3. Describe how these attractions make your relationship grow.

Prayer Point/Take Away for Today:
Thank God for my spouse!

Notes/Responses/Action:

-2-

DATING AFTER THE WEDDING

Read: Genesis 24:57–67

Focus: Note the progression of an arranged marriage. Deeply devoted love occurred *after* marriage in this scripture! Continue dating!

There are two fundamental reasons why dating is practiced in the Western world. One, to discover what the opposite gender is like. This is the beginning of establishing meaningful communication between two very different people. Woman and men generally communicate in rather different ways.* More about this later.

Two, learning to have fun with someone unlike ourselves. Men tend to communicate and understand fun in fairly unique ways. Women communicate with each other and understand fun in their own ways. Dating amplifies these differences.

A successful relationship usually develops as a couple discovers how to communicate and have fun together. Dating couples often break up because they fail to learn how to communicate effectively with each other and/or just don't have fun together.

Married couples need to continue dating each other. Why? For the same reasons unmarried couples date, but at a deeper

4

level. It is important to draw away from the routines of life and talk beyond the trivialities of living. Having fun together tends to re-invigorate the relationship.

Dating in the early stages of marriage may need special consideration since newly married couples often experience limited financial resources to splurge on dates. Creative dating does not necessarily have to result in large expenditures of money. Many married couples have discovered all sorts of fun things to do that cost little to nothing. These couples did whatever took them away from the hum-drum of daily living.

Brainstorm about ways you can have fun together. God gave you creativity. Use your creativity to find ways to enjoy dating each other!**

Resources:
You Just Don't Understand, Deborah Tannen, Ballantine Books.
**2002 Romantic Ideas*, Cyndi Haynes and Dale Edwards, Adams Media Corporation.

Discussion Questions:
1. Describe how each of you defines fun.

2. Make a list of fun things you can do together. Be creative!

3. What fun thing would you like to do together this week?

Prayer Point/Take Away for Today:
This week, we will remember a fun thing/event we did together before we were married. Then we will make time to retry this.

Notes/Responses/Action:

(Continued)

Notes/Responses/Action:

SOULMATES

Read: Genesis 24:1–67; Ephesians 5:31–33

Focus: The Genesis passage is one of the most interesting love stories in the Old Testament. It involves an amazing account of how God directed Abraham's servant to discover Rebekah and bring her to marry Isaac. The verses in Ephesians are the crowning summary of how a married couple is to relate to each other. And they probably include the best definition of soulmates found in the Bible.

There are few teachings in the Bible about whom you should marry. The lineage leading to Jesus from Abraham and King David had to be preserved, so those marriages were recorded by Matthew and Luke. Jewish people have traditionally held to the Old Testament standard where God told the Israelites not to marry the Gentiles living in the Promised Land because this would draw people away from God.

New Testament Christians were encouraged to marry believers. To those already married to non-believers, St. Paul generally discouraged divorce since the Christian's faithfulness might result in conversion of the spouse.

The New Testament is all about fulfilling the will of God in our lives as we allow Jesus to be our Lord. The emphasis of Christian scriptures is on pursuing a life reflecting the image of Jesus. Ephesians 5:31–33 seems to be about two people assisting each other in fulfilling God's will. In today's language, the two are to become soulmates.

Discussion Questions:

1. What does it mean to you to become more like Jesus?

2. In what ways are you assisting each other in fulfilling the will of God in your lives?

3. What additional soulmate qualities would you like to develop in yourself?

Prayer Point/Take Away for Today:

To think about my responsibilities as my spouse's soulmate.

Notes/Responses/Action:

(Continued)

Notes/Responses/Action:

BASIC NEEDS

Read: James 2:18, 3:13

Focus: Our actions need to match what we say. How we relate to each other is key to building a solid relationship.

Those who study human behavior often note the basic relational needs we all possess.* To be a soulmate, meeting the needs of your spouse, is key to developing a happy and fulfilling relationship. There are **five basic needs** that spouses have, and these are not usually met just because you said "I do." Time and hard work are required to help each other in all these areas.

Don't be discouraged if you find yourself doing less than your spouse might need in a particular area. Marital growth in meeting each other's needs should take place throughout your relationship. You might realize and agree that growth is the only sign of life. Grow throughout life. As you reflect on these basic needs of your spouse, start to think about how you can be partners in your growth as individuals and as a couple.

Physical needs: Beyond our needs for water, food, shelter, etc., the physical presence of others is essential in our lives. As previously mentioned, we are often attracted by the appearance of someone. But our physical appearance changes. Wrinkles appear! Gravity works on our bodies, and various features so attractive in our 20s give way to sagging! Change will happen, but the amazing thing is this: physical attraction can last a lifetime if emotional, mental, social, and spiritual needs are met.

In a marital relationship, you must satisfy many physical needs of the other person. Sexual intimacy is designed to help bond you together. Equally important is your service to each other. This spans a wide spectrum and includes meal preparation, laundry, home and vehicle maintenance, child care, household cleaning, and a host of other needs both of you must deal with on a daily basis. Many of these needs are not very romantic. Although such needs are essential, they can serve as a strong relational bond that makes romance more likely!

Life can settle into a routine, and it is all too common to take each other's physical needs for granted. Meeting your spouse's needs as time passes is very important. Honest discussion about your expectations and personal concerns can go a long way toward helping each other meet the demands of life. More about these concerns in later devotionals.

Emotional needs: Each person needs to feel loved, and your spouse is the most important person with this need. Love is locally defined, that is, everyone recognizes love in their own way. Later, we will discuss these love needs in detail. To meet your partner's emotional needs in a relationship requires that you maintain focus and be sensitive to what he/she is all about. Love is not satisfied once a week or only on Valentine's Day. We are all needy people, and meeting the love needs of each other is one of our most important relational concerns in marriage. Ask questions often. Never accept "fine" or "okay" as a response to a question.

Mental or brain needs: Everyone needs mental stimulation in some form. Discover what stimulates the brain of your spouse and feed that domain. The range of mental interests is wide: reading, finances, sports, academics, building, art, music, crafts, hobbies, repairs, or whatever. Encourage each other to develop brain

11

activities. If you have something in common here, emphasize that to build a relational connection. You might take a class together at the local community college. Build something together. The more you can connect mentally, the stronger will be your bond.

Social needs: No one is an island, and the same is true for a couple. Make connections with other couples. Develop group connections. Become part of a church couples' small group. In addition, encourage each other to connect with others of your gender, a political organization, a service club, or some group that interests you personally. This helps prevent you from being too dependent on each other.

Spiritual needs: Develop your spiritual life by sharing devotional and prayer times together. Encourage individual spiritual development. Attend and become involved in church and other organizations with a spiritual emphasis. Spiritual bonding can be a powerful glue to hold your relationship together, especially during difficult times.

Resource:
*http://booksums.blogspot.com/2008/04/mars-and-venus-on-date-john-gray.html

Discussion Questions:
1. Describe how you are meeting some of the physical, emotional, mental, social, or spiritual needs of each other.

2. How can I meet more of your needs?

3. What is your most pressing need right now?

Prayer Point/Take Away for Today:
What can I do to better meet my spouse's needs today?

Notes/Responses/Action:

-5-

FAITH FACTORS

Read: Matthew 22:37–39

Focus: The challenge of life and your relationship is to live out these amazing commandments.

How important is faith in a marital relationship? According to St. Paul and the Bible in general, having a life partner who is a believer is very important. If your personal faith is a significant part of your life, then being able to share your spiritual life with your spouse is integral to a happy relationship.

Why is this important? For Christians, the spiritual life is more than an add-on to life as a whole. Faith is the foundation on which all of life is based. Christians view our earthly lives as a place to show love to others and emulate the life of Jesus.

What is involved in the spiritual life? As a person who has personally accepted Jesus Christ as your personal Savior, the new life God gives you is one that involves faith with the Holy Spirit as your guide. Common features of a Christian believer's life include: reading the Bible, praying, interacting with other believers, and involvement in some outreach activity of service through a church, other charitable organization, school programs, or a wide variety of groups.

How compatible should you and your spouse be spiritually? Everyone comes from a different background. Take a look at your own spiritual background. Did your family of origin pray together? If so, was family prayer at a devotional time, at meals, at special events, rarely, or never?

Consider Bible reading and study. How were you raised in this area of spiritual development? How have you grown since then? One of the especially meaningful activities that Christian couples can experience is a shared devotional time. This typically includes scripture reading and prayer. A devotional book or guide can help.

How was church attendance treated when you were growing up? Do you and your spouse attend the same church or denomination? There is more than the name on the church door that fosters spiritual oneness in a marital relationship.

In terms of service to others, what was this like in your family of origin? What was the worldview in your home? How did your family view people, especially people unlike themselves racially, politically, culturally, or economically?

You and your spouse should not be clones of each other. That would be boring! But your faithfulness to God and concern for the world and its people are important characteristics that you can share as you grow spiritually.

Discussion Questions:
1. Describe the spiritual background of the family you grew up with. How did these experiences affect your spiritual life?

2. How do we each approach spiritual growth?

3. What changes might be helpful in our spiritual development as individuals, as a couple, and/or as a family?

Prayer Point/Take Away for Today:
How can I strengthen my spiritual life?

Notes/Responses/Action:

(Continued)

Notes/Responses/Action:

-6-

FAITH FACTORS: PRAYER

Read: Matthew 6:6–13, 18:19–20; Luke 5:16; John 15:7–8; 1 Thessalonians 5:16–18; James 4:3; 3 John 2

Focus: Prayer is a key part of the Christian life.

We are heavily influenced by our backgrounds. The norm is what we have experienced. If prayer was a significant factor in your first family, then that ripples through the lives and families of all participants — sometimes in a positive way and sometimes negatively.

Prayer is a conversation between you and God. Think about significant conversations you have experienced with other people. What were they like? Did you ask something of the other person and do all the talking? Did you take time to listen and consider what the other person said? Consider your conversation with God in a similar way.

How you talk with God is a conversation involving elements of the Lord's Prayer, which include: praise, wanting God's Kingdom to rule, and requests about important matters. How might this approach impact prayer in your personal life, in your life as a couple, and in your family?

Discussion Questions:
1. Take a look back at your family of origin in terms of prayer. How did your family's treatment of prayer impact and shape your own attitude toward prayer?

2. In your family of origin, did you depend on others to do the praying for you, or did you assume personal responsibility to pray? **Note**: This doesn't necessarily refer to prayers spoken aloud in the presence of others.

3. Were you taught to pray, for example, at bedtime? Or, if your parents were believers, did they assume you would somehow catch on to how to pray?

4. How do you react to prayer now? Think about your personal prayer life. How would you evaluate it? Do you feel reasonably satisfied with your prayer experiences?

5. As a couple, how does prayer impact our relationship? Is there a particular time that we pray together? Do we pray separately by ourselves?

6. Are we reasonably satisfied with our prayer in a family setting (if there are children)? If not, are there changes that might be appropriate?

7. Talk to each other about what concerns you today. Take time to pray together about those concerns.

Prayer Point/Take Away for Today:
I will pray specifically for concerns of my spouse and family.

Notes/Responses/Action:

(Continued)

Notes/Responses/Action:

(Continued)

Notes/Responses/Action:

FAITH FACTORS: THE SCRIPTURES

Read: 2 Timothy 3:15–16

Focus: The Bible is the source of God-knowledge throughout the history of the Hebrews and the Christian Church.

The ancient Hebrews treated the Old Testament scriptures with great reverence, even to the point of adorning themselves with words from important sections. The Old Testament was the "Bible" of the Hebrews and considered the authoritative source for their religious life.

Early Christians found in the Old Testament the evidence that Jesus was the Messiah or Christ, the Son of God. New Testament writers described the life and teachings of Jesus, as well as how the early Church began. Significant contributors, such as St. Paul, clarified how new believers in Jesus should live in the light of God's revelation of Himself in Christ. Study of both the Old and New Testaments has been the hallmark of believers ever since the assembly of the Christian scriptures.

Because the writers of the scriptures spoke and wrote in ancient languages not studied by most of us today, translators have worked hard to allow us to understand the meaning of these "God-breathed" words. It matters little which translation of the Bible you use. The goal of some translations is to come as close to "word-for-word" as can be done when translating from one language to another. Others translators try to present the meaning in words that you and I can identify with in our culture

As an individual, think about how you use the scriptures in your spiritual development. Some like to read the Bible through in a year, and there are helpful methods available to assist you in doing this. Others take the "random" search method of opening the Bible and reading whatever their eyes fall on.

Some use a devotional book as a launch pad to read a section of scripture along with a thought (sort of like this book you are reading). Others like to use topical approaches and focus on a theme, such as forgiveness. Some like to read a section of the Bible and stop when they find something that applies directly to them, and then meditate on that verse or verses. The possibilities are endless.

Discussion Questions:
1. How has the way your childhood family approached the Bible affected your approach to the Bible today?

2. How do you personally like to study the Bible?

3. How has the study of the Bible impacted your life?

4. How has the study of the Bible affected us as a couple? Do we study the Bible together? If not, how might a study of the scriptures be valuable to us?

5. How has the Bible impacted our family life, if we have children? What changes in Bible study, if any, would assist in the spiritual development of our family?

Prayer Point/Take Away for Today:
Find a Bible passage and read it aloud slowly, letting its meaning seep into your life. Ask God to reveal His truth to you.

Notes/Responses/Action:

-8-

FAITH FACTORS: OTHER BELIEVERS

Read: Acts 1:14, 2:42; Hebrews 10:25

Focus: The early Christians realized how important it is to share with fellow believers.

Everyone has a different personality, likes different things, and feels comfortable in different settings. Regardless of how much a person may be introverted or extroverted, most of us understand that we are not "islands." We need human contact.

We may not like crowds, but interacting with others in meaningful ways provides a degree of comfort and a sense of well-being. When Jesus sent out His disciples, they were in groups of two. Why? Because everyone needs the support of another, especially when confronted with problems or issues.

That is certainly one of the primary reasons for marriage. It is also why the Church, as a group of people meeting together for spiritual development, dates from the very first days of Christianity.

Discussion Questions:
1. How committed to a church were your parents? Did they shift from one congregation to another, trying to find a good fit? When things got dicey at church, what were the reactions of your

parents? How did you feel, as a result of the commitment to a church or lack thereof by your parents?

2. Growing up, what was church like for you? What sort of commitment did you feel to a particular local congregation, denomination, etc.?

3. Considering our present situation, how would we describe the ways our family interacts with other believers? How do other believers impact us and our family?

4. Are there changes we could make with how we relate to other believers that might improve the spiritual development of each of us and our family?

Prayer Point/Take Away for Today:
We will evaluate our relationship to a group of believers/church.

Notes/Responses/Action:

(Continued)

Notes/Responses/Action:

-9-

FAITH FACTORS: SERVICE

Read: Acts 6:1–7; 1 Corinthians 12:4–6; James 2:14–18

Focus: The early church understood the importance of non-clergy in the success of spreading the Christian faith.

When Jesus interacted with others, He acted out of compassion for people. This principle of living has been a trait fostered by believers from the early days of the Church. Helping others has been a guiding concept for Christians throughout the history of the faith.

Helping involves a wide range of volunteer activities. From teaching children on Sunday mornings to coaching basketball in a church league to working with the poor to sweeping floors, there is no limit to the acts of service available to believers. Many do volunteer work outside formal church settings as an outreach to the community where they live. We each have gifts. God's Spirit can use us for service. This can be valuable for the spiritual development of everyone in the family.

Discussion Questions:
1. How were you raised, in terms of doing acts of service for others? Were your parents active volunteers? How did their approach to service affect you during your growing up years?

2. Describe activities that impacted others when you have been personally involved. How did this make you feel?

3. Concerning our family today, how do we look upon service, in terms of developing our spiritual lives?

4. Have you ever experienced "spiritual burnout" as a result of being too busy with a volunteer schedule? How did you deal with this problem?

5. How might overcommitment impact our family? What is an appropriate level of service to others that becomes a vital part of our spiritual growth but without negatively affecting our family?

Prayer Point/Take Away for Today:
I will evaluate the things I do as service. What things do I need to change, add, or drop, and why?

Notes/Responses/Action:

(Continued)

Notes/Responses/Action:

-10-

FORGIVENESS

Read: Matthew 18:21–26; Ephesians 5:25–31

Focus: Jesus taught virtually unlimited forgiveness between believers. Paul taught that sacrificial forgiveness is part of the marital bond.

No one is perfect. If you expect your spouse to be perfect, then they should expect you to be perfect, too! You will both be disappointed if you try to play the "you be perfect" game! Better to look with curiosity toward your spouse and seek to understand him/her.*

How forgiving are you toward your spouse? We are all imperfect beings and need to live with the forgiveness attitude of Jesus. In response to how many times we should forgive the same person, Jesus gave an outlandish number: 490 times! In no way did Jesus want us to count up to 490 and then stop forgiving. He was teaching the principle of forgiveness that was so missing in the culture of His day. Since God has an infinite capacity to forgive, we are to emulate God by living a life of forgiveness.

Jesus went on to say that we should love others in the way we have been loved by God and that we should love ourselves as well. That also translates to forgiveness for others and ourselves. The underlying basis for Christianity is the self-sacrifice of Jesus for us. God loved us so much that He did death for our forgiveness.

31

So, when it comes to forgiving your spouse, the standard is straightforward: Jesus' forgiveness of you. The next time you have forgiven 489 times, pause and forget about counting!

There is a word that comes into play here: *grace*. Philip Yancey describes God's grace this way: "Grace means that no mistake we make in life disqualifies us from God's love ... Grace is irrational, unfair, unjust, and only makes sense if I believe in another world governed by a merciful God who offers another chance."** If grace is applied between two people, think how amazing the relationship can be!

Jesus did **not** intend for anyone to take advantage of another's forgiveness for their own benefit. When purposeful injury — whether physical, mental, emotional, or you name it — is put on another, this is wrong and requires admission and change on the part of the perpetrator.

Sacrificial living goes both ways! You might try to out-forgive your spouse, but don't ever think of forgiveness as a competition! We can never compare our forgiveness with the immensity of God's grace and forgiveness.

Resources:
The 7 Habits of Highly Effective People, Stephen R. Covey, A Fireside Book, Simon and Schuster (Chapter 5: Seek first to understand, then to be understood).
**Grace Notes,* Philip Yancey, Zondervan.

Discussion Questions:
1. Describe your understanding of forgiveness.

2. What part does forgiveness play in our marriage?

3. Is there something we could do to improve our approach to forgiveness?

Prayer Point/Take Away for Today:
Is there someone I need to forgive? What can I do now to begin that process of forgiveness?

Notes/Responses/Action:

-11 -

ABUSE ISSUES

Read: 1 Peter 3:8–9

Focus: The Christ-like response to problems is never abusive.

We all have backgrounds that are anything but perfect. Some have seriously abusive backgrounds.* The abuse may have involved physical violence, emotional or mental abuse, sexual exploitation/pornography, and/or substance abuse (drugs, alcohol, and tobacco).

Ignoring these abusive issues is unwise and can be dangerous. Abusive language and bullying are common experiences many of us have suffered in school. To become involved in promiscuous sex is not an uncommon peer pressure in schools.

Sex imposed by older relatives on children can be devastating in the memory of the exploited. Experimentation with addictive substances of all kinds can induce prolonged dependence and ruin physical, emotional, and mental health.

Have each of you moved on from those negatives, or is there unresolved baggage?

If you or your spouse is plagued by any abusive issue and have not sought or found help, then the wise thing to do is find a healthcare provider, organization, support group, or counselor to assist in dealing with issue(s). Otherwise, abusive backgrounds can color lives for years. Trying to go it alone is unwise. Support is very important.

Resources:
*https://www.healthline.com/health/mental-health/effects-of-emotional-abuse#find-a-professional
*https://www.drugabuse.gov/publications/health-consequences-drug-misuse/mental-health-effects

Discussion Question:
1. Are there abusive issues, past or present, which you feel would be appropriate to discuss with each other?

Alert: If there are unresolved abusive issues, seek professional help.

Prayer Point/Take Away for Today:
Do I have unresolved abusive issues that I need to deal with?
If so, what are my next steps in beginning that process?

Notes/Responses/Action:

(Continued)

Notes/Responses/Action:

-12-

VIOLENCE

Read: James 3:17–18; Proverbs 3:31; 1 Timothy 3:3

Focus: Christians avoid violence.

Violence is a topic that no one wants to think about in a marriage. The widespread physical abuse that occurs in some relationships, however, demands that the problem not be ignored.

Suppression of one gender for the benefit of the other has been all too common throughout human history. In most cultures, women have received the brunt of such abuse. You have probably seen this portrayed again and again in movies and television.

Violent tendencies can occur in either gender, but societal acceptance of gender dominance too often fosters expressions of violence by men more often than by women. Think how long it has taken in a democratic society like the United States for women to be allowed to vote and gain a variety of social, economic, and political equalities and independence.

In Western cultures, abuse has become less acceptable. Because of this more restrictive environment, violence may not show its ugly head until *after* the marriage ceremony. Potentially abusive persons may appear very nice during courtship. This may only delay violent expressions. How many have said, "If I only knew what kind of a person you were before we were married." The wedding ceremony conveys no "magic whiffle dust" that the pastor sprinkles on either partner to do away with problems or issues!

Fortunately, there is professional help for abusers, but they must be willing to accept it. Change can be slow and difficult. Sometimes the abuser was abused as a child or teen. This may require significant professional intervention to resolve.

For the abused person, the threat to leave the relationship often follows a tortuous path. The abuser may blame the abused for her/his behavior or may threaten him/her if she/he leaves. These threats may involve financial, emotional, or physical responses.

If the abused leaves, apparent penitence by the abuser may be accompanied by promises to change. Too often, the abuse returns. The most extreme situations do occur. Fifty percent of the women murdered in the U.S.A. are killed by intimate partners; only 12 percent are murdered by strangers.*

Of course, women can physically abuse men. I have heard of some pretty wicked physical abuse by women! Men kill women for a variety of reasons, but jealousy is a common one. Women tend to murder for financial or "love" reasons.**

All this discussion may seem morbid, but abuse is far too common to ignore. More than likely, you do not personally experience violence in your marriage, and that is wonderful. But it is important to be aware that certain behaviors may cause the buildup of resentment and can lead to unwanted responses. Do your part in maintaining a happy, peaceful marriage.

Resources:
*www.theatlantic.com/health/archive/2017/07/homicides-women/534306/ **
**www.abc.net.au/news/2018-02-05/female-murderers-more-likely-motivated-by-love-financial-gain/9378404

Discussion Questions:

1. What are some hints that a person might be violently abusive?

2. What part might faith play in dealing with someone who is physically abusive?

Note: If there is a history of violence in your family of origin that you want to discuss, it might be best to do this in the presence of a counselor.

Prayer Point/Take Away for Today:
I will be vigilant to protect and save my family from violence.

Notes/Responses/Action:

(Continued)

Notes/Responses/Action:

-13-

ABUSIVE WORDS

Read: Proverbs 12:16–19; Colossians 4:6; Ephesians 4:29

Focus: Use positive words, never abusive ones.

Abuse takes many forms. The more subtle abuse that is far too common involves the use of words. **Note:** The following comments about gender differences are highly generalized.

Women may be more likely to use this form of abuse very expertly on men. This can be devastating to a male partner.

Verbal abuse is not the same as goofy banter that men may engage in between themselves. But if a wife brings down a barrage of negative words on her husband, this can be very damaging to their relationship. Of course, men can also dump verbally abusive language on their wives. Verbal abuse knows no gender restriction.

Words are the most efficient and clearest form of human communication. Well-chosen words can hinder or help the connection between people. The largest use of words is a source of power in a relationship. Women tend to use many more words in a day than most men do. On the contrary, men can be highly skilled in the use of words.

How many marriages have ended due to the misuse of words? A thought can be communicated effectively or ineffectively by how well the speaker chooses his/her words.

Power in a couple's relationship resides with this very use or disuse of words.

John Gottman* has shown that the number of positive versus negative experiences which a couple has when they are together has an enormous impact on the toxicity or health of the marital relationship. He says that there must be **at least five times as many positive versus negative interactions** for a marriage to be successful.

Monitoring your positive to negative ratio of comments you make to your spouse is very important. Caustic comments are negative. Build-up comments are positive. We don't tire of sincere, positive comments. We become weary with negative ones.

And repetition is important! You can't tell each other that you love her/him once and forget to repeat this for a month! People need to hear sincere affirmation on a frequent basis.

Resource:
The Seven Principles for Making Marriage Work, John D. Gottman and Nan Silver, Crown Publishers.

Discussion Questions:
1. How do men relate positive thoughts to other men?

2. How do women relate positive thoughts to other women?

3. What are examples of positive versus negative words that couples give to each other?

4. How can we be more positive to each other?

Prayer Point/Take Away for Today:
I will say positive things to her/him today.

Notes/Responses/Action:

-14-

SELF-IMAGE

Read: Genesis 1:27; Luke 6:45

Focus: God's plan for us is to build each other up.

More about positive versus negative words: how important are these comments to our image of ourselves? Except for narcissists, people often tend to put themselves down in conversations. We rarely applaud ourselves because we are afraid this looks like self-conceit or self-aggrandizement. Since we don't speak well of ourselves for fear of being misunderstood, we often brush aside positive comments that come our way.

Negativity damages our self-image. That is why we need the five-to-one ratio of positive versus negative interactions observed by Gottman.* This means that one of the most important things a couple can do to enhance their relationship is tell the truth about positive aspects of their partner's life and attitude. Without being gushy or artificial, be honest in your praise of your spouse. He/she receives plenty of negativity, so a good dose of positive feedback does no harm.

Saying positive things helps offset negative experiences. Positive comments can insulate and heal her/him relative to negative words from whatever the source. If the boss chewed out him/her, the last thing you want to do is add more pain to his/her life. Your positive words and actions can build up her/his self-worth and offset much of what has been inflicted outside the home.

Home should be a refuge from whatever is damaging outside the family. Each of us needs to see ourselves as God sees us: "If God is for us, who can be against us?" (Romans 8:31b). You are the primary person who can bring God's love into focus for your spouse. Ask yourself, "Will what I say build her/him up or put her/him down?"

And remember Genesis 1:27. You are both made in the image of God, and you are here for a purpose!

Resource:
The Seven Principles for Making Marriage Work, John D. Gottman and Nan Silver, Crown Publishers.

Discussion Questions:
1. What are examples of how someone has built up your self-image?

2. Ask each other about positive things you can do to build up the other's self-image.

3. How do we avoid being insincere when giving positive comments to each other?

Prayer Point/Take Away for Today:
How can I build up her/his self-image?

Notes/Responses/Action

(Continued)

Notes/Responses/Action:

-15-

PERSONALITY

Read: Luke 6:37; Romans 14:12–13; 2 Peter 1:5–7

Focus: Accept each other for who you are.

Personality is an amazing combination of our genetics and our experiences. Studies of twins suggest that identical twins share about half of the same traits. On the other hand, fraternal twins share about 20 percent of the same traits.*

Many studies indicate that much of our personality structure is fairly firmly fixed. So trying to drastically change another person is not likely to have much positive effect. In fact, trying to change someone can be downright irritating. Intentionally trying to change another person's personality traits is almost universally unwise. On the other hand, modifications that are environmental and related to many factors — such as age, maturity, continuity of roles, etc. — can take place.*

We all have certain tendencies, and being aware of these is important for married couples. Many personality terms are part of our everyday vocabulary, e.g., introvert versus extrovert. If you are an outgoing person who loves to be with lots of people and your significant other is a homebody who is uncomfortable in crowds, you probably already know that being married didn't change much of anything about her/his tendency.

47

Perhaps the best you can hope for is to follow a general concept which works much of the time: **Give your spouse the gift of your opposition.**

For the extrovert, if you want to go out after working all day, say something like this to your introverted spouse: "I want to go out but, because I love you, I will stay home and enjoy an evening together." Of course, this allows the introvert to learn to say: "I'd really love to stay at home, but because you mean so much to me, let's go out and be with friends."

Give each other the **gift of your opposite tendency**. Be aware that the homebody will likely be exhausted after an intense group social event. And the outgoing person may feel a bit cramped staying at home. If you try to use the opposition idea, don't keep track of whose turn it is!

Resource:
*https://www.verywellmind.com/are-personality-traits-caused-by-genes-or-environment-4120707

Discussion Questions:
1. Describe yourself in terms of extrovert and introvert characteristics.

2. How might you give each other the "gift of your opposition"?

Prayer Point/Take Away for Today:
I will do something that my spouse loves but I have difficulty doing.

Notes/Responses/Action:

(Continued)

Notes/Responses/Action:

-16-

INTERESTS: SIMILAR OR DIFFERENT?

Read: Proverbs 12:25

Focus: Kindness is never out of style.

When you first began dating, perhaps you said, "We have so much in common! This must be right!" What did this mean? Did you like the same sports? Or the same kinds of movies? Or the same fast food?

Let's return to the contrast between extroverts and introverts. Perhaps the most obvious contrast is how each likes to spend her/his free time. Introvert personalities tend to prefer doing things with a party of one or two, at the most. Their common leisure activities often include watching TV/movies, doing a hobby or craft, working in a shop or garden, reading, repairing cars/house/appliances, etc. An extrovert's preferred leisure time is often spent with groups of people, going out, and anything that involves interaction with more than a couple of individuals.

Many people are neither pure introverts nor pure extroverts. This translates into enough variations and contrasts for lots of interesting differences.

Discussion Questions:
1. Discuss your personality differences in terms of interests.

2. If we experience significant contrasts in personality, how are we doing in learning to understand our differences and allowing each other to express those differences in his/her own way?

3. Besides giving the "gift of your opposition," what other ways can we resolve or mute tensions related to personality?

Prayer Point/Take Away for Today:
I will ask my spouse if I can do something with her/him that I usually do not do.

Notes/Responses/Action:

(Continued)

Notes/Responses/Action:

HABITS: LIFE'S DETAILS

Read: Proverbs 11:11–13; Romans 12:2; Matthew 7:12

Focus: Be adaptable to your spouse's neutral habits.

You may have heard that we all need habits so we can concentrate on the important things in life. That is probably true; however, habits can also place a strain on a couple's relationship. Habits are largely learned. We began learning them as infants. Habits come in three styles: good, neutral, and bad.

Bad habits may be illegal, immoral, unhealthy, damaging to others or ourselves, and are often easily seen and identified by other people, regardless of whether we see them in ourselves. Good habits are just the opposite. Friends and relatives may recognize them, and hopefully, we recognize them in ourselves. On the good to bad spectrum of habits, most habits are in the middle or neutral zone, neither good nor bad.

The huge set of habits in the middle can provide most of the daily frustrations and tensions in a relationship. To resolve these sorts of discomforts related to habit differences, it is important to have open and honest, but not angry, discussions. For example, I learned from my fiancée that doorknobs were not designed to be clothes hangers. That piece of knowledge saved some confrontations after we were married, maybe even on our wedding night! I discovered an amazing thing: I can change a habit!

Because we learn them, most habits can be modified, changed, dropped, or added to our repertoire of behaviors. Such things as how we sort or don't sort socks, leave the cap on or off a tube of toothpaste, or a host of other minute details of life are not particularly life-threatening. So we may tend to let these irritations go, rather than discuss them together in a calm and reasoned manner. But a direct discussion can gently relieve a pond full of frustrations and prevent the dam from breaking to allow an overflow of emotion that clouds our relationship.

We are not talking about true obsessive-compulsive disorder (OCD), which is a condition of excessive or repetitive behavior that departs from simple habit. Such situations may require a therapist for help.

A marital relationship involves giving up some things and taking on others. Habits play an important role in this give-and-take process. You can't solve all habit issues at once, but continuing honest discussions can set the tone for dealing with bothersome habits as they arise under a variety of conditions.

Discussion Questions:
1. Describe habits of your own that might be irritating to your spouse. For starters, how do you begin and end your day? Be specific.

2. Respond to each other's habits in terms of how accepting you are of their actions.

3. Describe how resistive you are about changing your habits.

4. Select one of your spouse's slightly annoying habits and discuss it together. Don't assume this habit will change. Do assume that you might become more accepting and less frustrated with the habit.

Prayer Point/Take Away for Today:
What habit might I change, for my spouse's sake?

Notes/Responses/Action:

(Continued)

Notes/Responses/Action:

-18-

FAMILY OF ORIGIN

Read: Proverbs 25:19; 2 Timothy 1:5–7

Focus: Be sensitive to your spouse's background.

We are all products of many influences in our lives up to this point. Not the least of these is the home we grew up in. There is a truism that most counselors seem to agree on: **You do marry a family,** for good or ill. Initially, you may have resisted this statement but, on reflection, have come to realize how much the home you grew up in has influenced you.

Discussion Questions:
Spend time talking with each other about your homes of origin:

1. How were the genders treated in each of your families? Was there gender repression or lack of equality? Was anybody a doormat for other members of the family?

2. How were household chores handled?

3. What was the family conversation like around a dinner table? Or did the family eat together?

4. What things that you experienced in your families of origin have you left behind and why? What things have you kept from your family of origin and why?

Prayer Point/Take Away for Today:
I will think about something I do that comes from my family-of-origin which I am glad I embraced. Also, I will consider something I might like to drop.

Notes/Responses/Action:

(Continued)

Notes/Responses/Action:

MESSIES VERSUS CLEANIES

Read: Proverbs 15:33

Focus: When faced with differences, first be wise.

No one needs to define a *messie* or a *cleanie*; the words are self-explanatory. The differences are clear. It is also not a surprise that cleanies and messies often marry each other.

These patterns are partly learned but may grow out of certain personality types. There are lots of websites dealing with messies but very few on cleanies!

Sandra Fenton* describes some of the reasons behind messiness. She says messies often have high ideals, are well-educated and successful, with big ideas and ambition. This may grow out of perfectionism and can produce a lack of focus, fear of losing control, not having enough to help others, a desire to do only big jobs and not small ones, a sentimentality about throwing things out, and being visually tuned out to the local environment.

On the other side of the story, Fenton says cleanies express perfectionistic tendencies by needing order in their lives and environment. Often this is a characteristic dating from childhood when order was rewarded. Psychologists separate perfectionism from OCD, which is much more extreme in its behavioral manifestations.

Cleanies often clash with messies wherever there is a lack of cleanliness in a home, in how well-organized a room may be (unfolded clothes, randomly stacked magazines, etc.), and over anything related to planning or carrying out a plan.

Suggestions for messies and cleanies to live together in reasonable harmony involve various coping mechanisms. Here are a few offered by two psychologists:**

- Learn how to communicate and negotiate without insulting or cutting down your partner.

- Do not accuse, but ask to work on the problem.

- Set up messie and cleanie zones.

- Use your smartphone to set times for a project to be completed.

- Talk about why each is concerned or not concerned with an issue.

- There may be something in a person's background driving a particular behavior or concern.

- Don't take the differences personally. The situation may have nothing to do with you.

- If you can afford it, hire someone to clean your living space, if that will help.

- Above all, remember why you are together: you love each other!

Resources:
*www.imom.com/6-reasons-why-the-messie-is-messy/#.W-dJyeJRfcs
**www.today.com/health/study-reveals-how-neat-freak-slob-can-live-peace-924727

Discussion Questions:
1. Each describe yourself on the messie-cleanie spectrum.

2. What messie/cleanie issues have we experienced in the past? How were these resolved, if they were resolved?

3. Discuss ways we can deal kindly with messie-cleanie issues.

Prayer Point/Take Away for Today:
Am I a messie or cleanie? Should I modify my behavior?

Notes/Responses/Action:

(Continued)

Notes/Responses/Action:

-20-

WORDS: THE STUFF OF COMMUNICATION

Read: Psalm 19:14; Proverbs 16:24, 18:20, 20:15, 27:9

Focus: Choose your words wisely!

Words are the most important tools in your relationship toolbox. What you say and how you say it are key to developing a happy and fulfilling marriage. Using language to build connections pays big dividends.

Effective communication is not, contrary to popular thought, rocket science. There are innumerable books about how women and men communicate differently.* Boiling things down to the bare minimum, two things stand up and shout to us about how to communicate well. One, **listen to understand.** Two, **speak with the other person in mind.**

Speaking with the other person in mind means to be aware of what someone else will hear and how they may understand what you are saying. It is one thing to say something, but quite another to try to say it from the other person's point of view. Ask yourself: "How will she/he understand what I say?" This single approach can save a great percentage of misunderstandings and hurt feelings between couples.

To do this properly does take some thought, but since you know something about your spouse, you can craft your words so

64

you are clear. You can be aware of how your spouse may interpret or misinterpret your words. If you think your words will create anger, hurt, discouragement, or other negative feelings, you have the ability to pause and adjust how and what you will say. Perhaps you should say nothing! Sometimes, we should do what only humans can do: **wait before reacting, and then decide what to say, if anything.**

The other big part of effective communication is listening well. This can be a chore for some men. As an exercise, eavesdrop on a group of women talking. Then listen in as a group of men talk. Notice the difference? Generally, the women listen carefully and respond sympathetically to each other, unless somebody is mad at somebody else! The men may offer advice, whether asked for it or not, but are more likely waiting to jump into the conversation with a bigger or more powerful story than the previous speaker. These are quite generalized observations but not uncommon differences in genders.*

Men can learn a great deal by observing how a woman listens to another woman.* Notice there is usually very clear eye contact between women. Also, note the frequent reinforcing verbals: "Yes," "Really?", "My!", etc. Although it is irresponsible to try to convert men into women, most men can improve their conversations with women by keeping eye contact and letting her know you are still awake! A hint: rather than staring into both her eyes, focus on her left eye, which apparently affects the right side of her brain (recommended by a famous speaker and probably without scientific proof, but it seems to work and prevents her from becoming uncomfortable if you tend to stare).

If your conversations often end with frustration, try the above two approaches and note if things turn out better. Seeing things from the other person's point of view and paying attention as he/she speaks are gold when it comes to building your relationship.

Resources:

You Just Don't Understand, Deborah Tannen, Ballantine Books.

Men are from Mars, Women are from Venus, John Gray, HarperCollins Publishers.

The Seven Principles for Making Marriage Work, John M. Gottman and Nan Silver, Crown Publishers.

Discussion Questions:

1. How would you describe your word communication with each other? Take turns illustrating what speaks most effectively to you.

2. This week, how can I speak with your understanding in mind.

Prayer Point/Take Away for Today:

I will pay attention to what my spouse is saying. I may try the left eye approach!

Notes/Responses/Action:

(Continued)

Notes/Responses/Action:

WORDS: BUILD UP OR BREAK DOWN

Read: Matthew 7:3–5; 1 Peter 4:8

Focus: Say the good word.

Our words have huge power. They can build up a relationship or destroy it. Think of a TV drama or movie where you saw this happening. What approach destroyed the relationship? What resolved the problem and built up the relationship?

A careful analysis usually reveals some obvious mistakes or successes. Criticism and cynical words did *not* help. Flashes of anger and hotly spoken words that fried the other person were effective only at destroying the relationship.

On the other hand, admission of guilt or responsibility and requests for forgiveness were usually healing. Kind, thoughtful words blunted emotional outbursts and drew the persons together.

Simple solutions would have transformed negative experiences into positive ones. That is why **thinking before speaking** is so important. Some suggest counting to three before responding to a negative or irritating comment. Use your unique human ability to give some thought to what you might say.

Irrational outbursts of emotion-filled, angry words almost never do anything but defeat any attempt at solving a problem. But thoughtful, calm words tend to reduce the emotion of the moment and foster better understanding.*

Resource:
Why Marriages Succeed or Fail, John Gottman with Nan Silver, Fireside, Simon and Schuster.

Discussion Questions:
1. Think of successful or unsuccessful communication examples that you have experienced with each other.

2. How did you bring about resolution of the issue? If the problem was not resolved, what might be done to achieve a better outcome?

3. What might you do to improve your use of words with each other? Tell what words are especially important for you to hear.

Prayer Point/Take Away for Today:
What words can I use today that will encourage my spouse?

Notes/Responses/Action:

(Continued)

Notes/Responses/Action:

-22-

WORDS: FIX OR LISTEN

Read: Proverbs 18:13

Focus: Think before you answer an unasked question.

One of the most frustrating conversational methods that almost never works is to try and *fix* the other person's problem — unless a *repair* is requested. If someone is telling you about a problem, the answer or solution may be obvious to you. So the natural tendency is to break in and offer how you think she/he should solve the problem. If this has happened to you, it is no surprise that you may have been upset, especially if you hadn't finished telling your story!

Many people don't want your opinion of how to fix their problem! This may seem strange to you as a listener. Often, they just want to describe the issue and enlist your ability to listen to them. The truth is that often they can solve their own problems; they just need an audience to listen to their frustration.

Many of us like to wear the Mr./Mrs. Fixit Hat.* Why? Because, in our unfathomable wisdom, we can resolve things quickly and move on to the next subject. Here is the clue: your spouse may only want you to put on your Listening Cap and keep your solutions to yourself!

All this is set aside, however, *if* the person actually *requests* your opinion. Then you are free to carefully — and without seeming to be a know-it-all — discuss your thoughts on the subject. You might be able to help her/him.

If you are the one who wants to tell your story of frustration, you might let your eager Fixit person know that you just need a kind and attentive ear.

Resource:
*https://www.familiesonlinemagazine.com/couples/mr-fix-it.html

Discussion Questions:
1. How do you feel when someone breaks into your story with a fix-it approach? Share examples.

2. What can you do if you feel like you know the answer to someone's problem, but they don't ask your opinion?

Prayer Point/Take Away for Today:
I will avoid trying to fix my spouse. Instead, I will do more listening.

Notes/Responses/Action:

(Continued)

Notes/Responses/Action:

-23-

WORDS: NAGGING AND TELLING THE TRUTH

Read: Proverbs 21:9

Focus: No one likes to be nagged!

No one likes a nagger, someone who always seems to be harping on one flaw or another that we may or may not even know we have. Nagging may be funny in a TV program, but it is no fun in real life.

What is the problem with nagging? The universal response I have heard is: "It is irritating!"

Why does nagging bother us? Nagging usually focuses on some weakness that the nagger feels a need to address. Nagging is never requested, but it is spoken anyway! Naggers have the problem solved and want you to fix yourself or find someone who can help you.

Unfortunately, naggers often don't realize they are nagging. They are simply offering an observation and perhaps ways for you to use their observation of your behavior to shape up!

There is one underlying thought to consider if you feel that someone is nagging you. Perhaps there *might* be a seed of truth in the nag. That doesn't justify nagging! But it might pay to consider the nagger's words before writing them off completely.

The problem with nagging is that you may know there is some truth in what the person is saying, but you are offended by the nagger's approach. Their continual reminder really bugs you.

Nagging rarely works and often steels a person from making any changes that a nagger suggests, whether valid or not. If told they are nagging, the offender doesn't usually see it that way. After all, they believe that somebody needed to say that there is a problem!

Then there is the person who likes to "tell the whole truth." This may seem like a good thing, but such an approach often ends up looking a lot like nagging. Telling the whole truth is a misnomer and is usually just another excuse to nag.

Nagging does not build a relationship. Being honest in a relationship usually means telling the truth *gently*. Your tone of voice can make a big difference as to the outcome when you "tell the truth." Remember that people love a good listener. They never appreciate a nagger.

Discussion Questions:
1. Do a self-inspection. Have I nagged recently? If so, why? Share examples.

2. If you have felt nagged, how did it make you feel? Share examples.

3. What is a better way to communicate than by nagging?

Prayer Point/Take Away for Today:
I will think before saying something that might nag.

Notes/Responses/Action:

-24-

WORDS: EXPRESSING A NEED

Read: Proverbs 8:6–9

Focus: Be clear and accurate.

One of the more difficult pieces of communication is how to express a need without seeming to be selfish. Narcissism is a disorder that focuses on the self to an extreme. For a narcissist, the world revolves around her/him. So, if you have a specific need in a relationship, the last thing you usually want to do is appear to have this disorder.

Yet, your needs are real, and your spouse may not know what you need without being told. This is where it gets delicate. Words become very important when you express a need. Avoid any hint of selfishness; that would be counterproductive.

Expressing a need in a relationship is very important for both parties. Your goal is to understand each other and meet each other's needs. One approach is to express your need in terms of how this will build your relationship. This tends to blunt a misinterpretation that you are being purely selfish.

Marriage is a two-way street with both spouses giving and receiving benefits. The overall result should strengthen the bond you feel. Therefore, it is important to ask the other person about needs they may have that are not being met.

You can foster an atmosphere of mutual expression of needs by asking good questions. If neither knows what the other needs, then frustration and unhappiness can result. Say your need clearly and with humility, but never as an accusation.

Discussion Questions:

1. What ways are counterproductive when expressing a need?

2. Discuss an example of a need you have, which your spouse could meet, in terms of building your marital relationship.

Prayer Point/Take Away for Today:

I will express any need I have in a careful manner that is still honest.

Notes/Responses/Action:

(Continued)

Notes/Responses/Action:

-25-

WORDS: COMMUNICATING FEELINGS

Read: Proverbs 17:27

Focus: Say how you feel but with care.

Many studies* indicate that not everyone talks about their feelings as well as others do. Women are often more effective in using emotional language than many men are. To improve a man's ability to speak about his feelings, a woman may need to demonstrate by using words which convey how she feels. The object is not to make men into women. That would be a very bad thing! Instead, men can learn to understand the feeling language used by women and speak their own feelings better.

If a person is bottled up inside and can't express what is going on, then communication with a spouse is limited. Being able to describe the stresses of life verbally can be very freeing and can allow healing to take place. Men rarely speak feelings within their gender group, but can learn to talk openly with their spouses. This is a private matter and is one of the beautiful things about spousal communication.

The use of words to convey the stresses we feel can allow a couple to have a communication line that is unique and very positive for their relationship. This is one of the great benefits of marriage! Take advantage of feeling language by using some.

Resource:
*https://psychcentral.com/blog/6-ways-men-and-women-communicate-differently/

Discussion Questions:
1. Talk about the use of feeling words in your conversations. Give examples.

2. What are ways to express stresses in words?

3. What are ways to express happiness in words?

4. Describe how to respond to each other when you use feeling words.

Prayer Point/Take Away for Today:
I will listen for feeling words from my spouse and respond appropriately.

Notes/Responses/Action:

(Continued)

Notes/Responses/Action:

-26-

WORDS: HUMOR

Read: Proverbs 17:22

Focus: Good humor is healthy!

God gifts human beings with an amazing quality: humor. Laughter and amusement are second nature to us.

Laughing — not just smiling, but real "belly laughs" — provides huge health benefits.* One well-known individual, when he received the news of his serious illness, found all the funny movies he could and watched them. Apparently, he laughed himself back to health! This is not to construe that we should avoid physicians and hire comedians!

Women have told me many times that one of the important attractions drawing them to their spouse was: "He makes me laugh." Why is laughing so good for couples? Perhaps there is natural bonding as a result of this basic human characteristic of humor. Whatever the reason, please laugh out loud!**

But humor has its limits in a family. Avoid the sarcastic laughter involved when one of the family members is continually picked on in a derogatory manner. Perhaps all families have some in-house humor that comes out of a shared experience. No one else might see the humor, or perhaps it is so private that it is not shared outside the family.

A couple learned this lesson well as a result of a kitchen disaster. One was at work while the other ended up in a kitchen filled with burned food. On reciting the tale, the recipient of the catastrophe was anything but in a good humor. The spouse nodded with understanding and did not smile. After reciting the problem, the person saw the humor in the story and laughed. The listener could then laugh. When you laugh is critical. Don't laugh too soon! So, feel free to laugh out loud! It does a body good!

Resources:
*https://www.helpguide.org/articles/mental-health/laughter-is-the-best-medicine.htm
**https://news.ku.edu/2015/08/27/first-comes-laughter-then-love-study-finds-out-why-humor-important-romantic-attraction

Discussion Questions:
1. Take turns describing your ability to laugh.

2. What kind of humor do you enjoy most?

3. Tell a funny story about yourself.

Prayer Point/Take Away for Today:
I will laugh at something I have done.

Notes/Responses/Action:

(Continued)

Notes/Responses/Action:

-27-

WE ARE ALL A LITTLE WEIRD

Read: Proverbs 27:6

Focus: Accept wise counsel, even when it hurts.

Everybody has quirks. A big key to a happy marital relationship is learning to accept each other, quirks and all. Nobody is without imperfections (just in case you were uncertain). Yet, our perfectionistic tendencies trick us into thinking that our spouse should not be a bit weird. Each of us is less than perfect.

What do you do when you learn this important fact? Perhaps the best thing to do is admit your own faults and learn to live with the faults of your spouse. Who can you change? Not your spouse! The best you can do is accept who you are and accept who she/he is. No use fooling ourselves into trying to fix any of the other person's weirdnesses. Just work on your own, and that may trigger a similar response in your spouse.

Acceptance is a wonderful virtue in a couple relationship. Know that many things will never change, so get over trying to twist her/him into your mold. Accept your spouse as he/she is and grow yourself, with God's help. After all, what alternative is there? This caveat is important: learn to live with the imperfections of each other.

Discussion Questions:

1. Take turns describing some of your own goofy quirks. Laugh together.

2. Talk about accepting each other and letting God work on each of you.

Prayer Point/Take Away for Today:

I will be more accepting of my spouse's uniquenesses.

Notes/Responses/Action:

-28-

LOVE LANGUAGE

Read: Proverbs 12:22; Colossians 3:14

Focus: Nothing beats love.

Gary Chapman* has probably done more to assist couples in understanding their differences and how to relate to each other than anyone can imagine. He observed that everyone has a primary way that they understand love. He calls this your *love language*. The five ways we recognize love are: **words of affirmation, quality time, receiving gifts, acts of service, or physical touch.** He also indicated that we have a secondary love language, and a third love language, etc. But one of these five ways is what we really recognize as someone expressing love to us.

If your spouse most enjoys spending quality time with you, then that is her/his *primary love language*. But if your personal love language is physical touch, then you may not understand her/his spending quality time with you as love. This contrast may leave each feeling less than really loved. Another example might be where one person loves to receive gifts, but their spouse recognizes words of affirmation as the big deal. They each understand a significant love event only when the activity fits their personal love language.

In order to express love to someone, it is important to do something that fits the language of love that is *primary* for them.

When your spouse goes out of her/his way to express your love language, you know it! The point is: different people have different love languages. When we learn someone's *primary love language* and behave toward them in that manner, then they feel loved.

The problem arises when we try to express our love language to someone who has a different love language. For example, suppose receiving gifts is your primary love language, but your spouse needs quality time as her/his primary love language in order to feel loved. If you give him/her a gift, he/she may acknowledge the gift but with little satisfaction. You may feel hurt that the gift was not well received. Both of you feel less than happy as a result of not interacting with the appropriate love languages.

Figuring out one's love language is not difficult. Go online to take an assessment or just make observations or talk about it with your spouse. Then, focus on giving your spouse what he/she recognizes as his/her primary love language. Both can be happy with the result. Once you understand someone's love language and respond in kind, that person feels loved.

I encourage both of you to read this very helpful book by Gary Chapman. (BTW: Reading a book together can open the door to great couple discussion starters.)

Note: Physical touch, as a love language, does not necessarily mean sex. You have probably known individuals who seem unable to speak without touching you. Physical touch is likely their love language.

Resource:
The Five Love Languages, Gary Chapman, Northfield Publishing.

Discussion Questions:
1. What do you think are/were the primary love languages of your parents?

2. Evaluate each of your love language(s).

3. Discuss how each of you can express your spouse's love language.

4. How might expressing each other's love language enhance our relationship?

5. You might try to understand your children's love languages and see how this impacts your relationship to each of them.

Prayer Point/Take Away for Today:
I will do my best to express my love based on my spouse's love language.

Notes/Responses/Action:

(Continued)

Notes/Responses/Action:

-29-

APOLOGY LANGUAGE

Read: Colossians 3:13

Focus: Forgiveness is essential.

Because we are human, we make mistakes and need to give an apology. Gary Chapman teamed with Jennifer Thomas* to discover the ways in which we recognize an apology. Like the five love languages, we understand an apology when it is couched in our appropriate language of apology. The five languages of apology are:

1. Expressing regret: "I'm sorry."

2. Accepting responsibility: "Know what? I was just plain wrong."

3. Making restitution: "I'd like to make this right between us. What can I do?"

4. Genuinely repenting: "That is something I don't want to do again."

5. Requesting forgiveness: "Can you forgive me, please?"

Note that the languages range from a fairly low level of regret to a high level of sorrow. The exact words to use are not significant, but expressing the idea needs to happen.

Since everyone understands apology in their own way, it is important to learn to express an apology in a manner that your spouse understands. Level one may not even be considered an apology for many people. They need to hear something at an upper level in the hierarchy of apology to understand the intent of the apology.

Resource:
The Five Languages of Apology, Gary Chapman and Jennifer Thomas, Northfield Publishing.

Discussion Questions:
1. Take turns describing what you consider as an apology.

2. Does the level of apology depend on the infraction? If so, how?

3. How have you apologized to each other in the past? How might you need to change in the future?

Prayer Point/Take Away for Today:
When I goof up, I will do my best to apologize using my spouse's apology language.

Notes/Responses/Action:

(Continued)

Notes/Responses/Action:

WHEN YOU ARE WRONG

Read: James 5:16a

Focus: Confession heals.

Since each of us understands apologies in a different way, it is important to recognize when you make an error and to make amends. Others see our actions and words from their perspective. We see them from our own bias.

Typically, we try to justify what we say and do by playing the *blame game*. This is easily done by throwing responsibility onto someone or something else: our spouse, a family member, our work environment, our boss, how we feel, sickness, the government, the church, you name it. Somebody besides me is the cause! This immature approach never solves the problem. Only when we can sing with sincerity the old song, "It's me, it's me, it's me, O Lord, standin' in the need of prayer" can we start to rebuild a broken or cracked relationship.

We are responsible for what we say and what we do. Oh, there are outside influences, to be sure, but the decisions that we make are our responsibilities. God has given us a totally unique ability, among all the millions of species on Earth: **we can choose what we will do.** Theologians call this *free will*. This powerful gift, combined with faith and prayer, can allow us to "move mountains," as Jesus said.

When we try to blame others, we shirk our ability to own what we do, and we mute the value of God's gift of choice. Breaking the cycle of throwing our bad behavior and words on others frees us from our natural tendencies and builds bridges connecting us with people we care about.

The bottom line: Admit when you are wrong, apologize, and move forward in your marital relationship. Confession opens the door for acceptance and healing.

Discussion Questions:
1. Why is it so difficult to admit when we are wrong? Share examples.

2. Describe a time when you admitted being wrong and what helped to resolve the issue.

3. When your spouse admits being wrong, what should your response be?

Prayer Point/Take Away for Today:
I will do my best to admit being wrong sooner than I usually do.

Notes/Responses/Action:

(Continued)

Notes/Responses/Action:

-31-

ANGER

Read: James 1:19–20; Ecclesiastes 7:9; Ephesians 4:26;
Proverbs 14:29, 15:1, 15:18, 19:11, 22:24-25, 29:11;
Psalm 19:14, 37:8; Colossians 3:8

Focus: Anger usually gets you nowhere that you want to go.

We are emotional beings. God gave us the ability to choose how to react when faced with danger. You have probably heard of *flight* or *fight* as the response choices we can make in a dangerous situation. That is the case for most organisms, but there is another approach open to human beings: *cooperation.* Jesus taught, when faced with an adversary, that His followers take this third approach.

How might cooperation look in a situation where a married couple faces off and anger reaches the danger point of harming the relationship? First of all, remember that anger is not, in itself, evil ("be angry and sin not," Ephesians 4:26). Jesus displayed anger when He drove out money changers from the Temple. So, anger is not the issue.

What we do with the anger is important.* In Proverbs, there is a significant statement: "A soft answer turns away wrath" (Proverbs 15:1). Many who try this approach find that it keeps disagreements from becoming destructive arguments. One author suggests that stretching your fingers, when you sense you are clinching your fists, also helps.

Probably the most important thing is to stop talking and analyze what you are doing. Pushing ahead when angry rarely resolves an issue. Another source recommends asking for a pause, then returning to the discussion later, perhaps in an hour, if possible.

Your posture is important in dealing with an emotionally charged topic. Sit side by side instead of facing each other. When you are beside and touching her/him, focus on the problem in front of you as opposed to thinking that your spouse is the problem. And always avoid those antagonizing "you" statements ("You always ___," You never ___"). Instead, use "I" statements ("When this happens, I feel ___"). And, above all, remember what you want to happen. You want to build a loving relationship, even when you disagree.

Note: If there are serious anger issues, it might be best to seek help from a counselor or therapist.

Resource:
*https://www.mayoclinic.org/healthy-lifestyle/adult-health/in-depth/anger-management/art-20045434

Discussion Questions:
1. Describe a recent heated discussion or argument you had with each other. How did you resolve the issue? If it is still smoldering, how might you go about solving the problem?

2. Describe a better way of resolving concerns that you have. If you resolved an argument so both were happy with the result, how can you repeat the method?

Prayer Point/Take Away for Today:
If I feel anger rising during a discussion with my spouse, I will pause and think before responding.

Notes/Responses/Action:

JEALOUSY

Read: Proverbs 6:30–35; Proverbs 27:4, 14:30; 1 Corinthians 3:3; 2 Corinthians 12:20; Galatians 5:19–20

Focus: The book of Proverbs presents an Old Testament description of contrasting emotions by comparing a thief to an adulterer. The Jewish "eye for an eye" is taken even further, which illustrates the power of jealousy. St. Paul's notes in the New Testament classify jealousy with some awful sins.

Jealousy in a relationship is an emotional powerhouse that can destroy the beautiful picture of marital happiness found throughout the Bible. There is a good form of jealousy and a bad form.* The good form involves commitment and protection of your relationship. The bad form is quite different and often involves feelings of inadequacy and unresolved issues.

Common causes that trigger the bad form of jealousy frequently revolve around real or imagined romantic connections between someone outside the marriage and one's spouse. To avoid this sort of trigger, both partners need to be discrete when interacting with a person of the opposite gender. Friendships are fine, but there are lines that cannot be crossed without setting the stage for misinterpretation and jealous feelings.

Once a line is transgressed, then restoring a couple's equilibrium can be difficult. Often, there was no intentional bad behavior, but inappropriate choices were made. It is often difficult to explain this away. Better to be safe than sorry. In many cases, seeing a third party counselor/pastor will help restore the relationship.

There is also the jealousy that comes when one partner is too consumed with work, volunteer service, church activities, etc. Open, honest discussions need to occur so the offended partner can voice her/his concerns. The jealousy here is usually not as intense as sexually-related jealousy, but the loneliness and disrespect created by too much outside commitment hurts deeply. This can provide a temptation to seek friendships outside the marriage that may turn into unfaithfulness. If this happens, the married couple should seek counseling and break off the outside contact.

The bottom line: Avoid the triggers that generate jealous feelings. If one partner is too possessive, however, then jealousy can lurk at the door, ready to disrupt an otherwise good relationship. Possessiveness may be indicative of other issues, such as prior problems with persons who cheated. Again, seek help from a pastor or counselor if the problem escalates.

Talking about your outside relationships and other commitments can cut off the triggers before they become a problem. Everyone wants to be in a relationship with someone who is faithful. Avoid the very appearance of wrong behavior (1Thessalonians 5:22).

Resource:
*https://www.focusonthefamily.ca/content/understanding-healthy-and-unhealthy-jealousy

Discussion Questions:

Note: Depending on the level of concern, some discussions might best take place with a counselor/pastor present.

1. If appropriate, discuss any concerns related to outside influences, regardless of the type.

2. How difficult would it be to forgive someone who is unfaithful?

3. What is needed to forgive an unfaithful person? Where does the grace of God enter?

Prayer Point/Take Away for Today:
Am I doing something that could create a jealousy problem for my spouse?

Notes/Responses/Action:

(Continued)

Notes/Responses/Action:

-33-

CONFLICT RESOLUTION

Read: James 1:19; Psalm 19:14; Proverbs 12:18, 18:13; Ephesians 4:29; Philippians 2:4; Colossians 3:13; 1 Peter 3:8–9

Focus: Resolving a conflict involves listening a lot and speaking less.

Resolving a conflict is perhaps one of the most important skills a couple can learn. Unfortunately, most couples enter marriage without training in this key area. Yet, the training is not high order learning! And learning to deal with conflict in a relationship is fundamental to keeping equilibrium in marriage.

The first thing to be very clear about is this: couples have conflicts! Some people, viewing a couple from the outside, might say, "Oh, they never argue. They are the perfect couple." Maybe not in public, but most couples have issues over which they may become quite emotional. So, expect conflicts to arise.

A conflict is not the problem. You both have opinions. Differences of opinion are normal in a marital relationship and can help the couple avoid mistakes.

As soon as you recognize the seed that can germinate into a conflict, kick into conflict-resolving mode. Otherwise, the emotional nature of a disagreement can escalate feelings to unhealthy levels.

Either one or both of you may realize that an issue is causing feelings to rise in temperature and should call for a pause in the discussion. Whoever recognizes this can start to turn down the heat by asking the basic question, "What are we arguing about?" It is very important for both to be on the same page; sometimes each of you is talking about something different!

Agree on what the issue is and talk about the perspective each of you brings to the discussion. How have you handled it in the past?

If you are both stumped about how to proceed or have difficulty seeing each other's views, agree to stop and start over from scratch. Take a piece of paper and create a list of things you might do to solve or resolve whatever you are talking about. Together, choose a likely scenario and decide together to work on this approach. Become collaborators to attack the problem rather than attackers of each other.

After you have each tried your part for resolution, discuss the results. Give high-fives with success or choose another solution to try.

Usually, something like the above approach can bring the emotional responses down and let your rational minds take over, while strengthening instead of weakening the relationship.*

Resource:
*https://www.amanet.org/training/articles/the-five-steps-to-conflict-resolution.aspx

Discussion Questions:

Note: If this topic is too emotion-charged, you may wish to seek help from a counselor or pastor, as appropriate.

1. Talk about a conflict you have had. How was it resolved or, if it was not resolved, how might you approach the issue to solve it using some of the ideas listed above?

2. What approach might work best for you to use to resolve conflicts in the future?

3. How do you feel after resolving a conflict?

Prayer Point/Take Away for Today:
The next time we have a conflict, I will pause and ask why we are arguing.

Notes/Responses/Action:

(Continued)

Notes/Responses/Action:

-34-

EATING

Read: Proverbs 23:6; 1 Corinthians 10:31

Focus: Let food be a calming influence.

Of all the things people do together, eating is a common denominator. In early times, families ate almost every meal together. Now, the rush of modern life makes eating three meals a day in each other's presence an impossible dream.

Food has the potential to bond people, but things can distract during a meal. Technology can be a distraction and should be put away, since this is often the only time when everyone can speak to the whole family group. Eating together provides an ideal time to discuss what each has done during the day, to share ideas, to ask and answer questions, and generally to see where everyone is in their lives.

Too often, the meal table has been used as a time for disciplining or chastising particular family members. Michael Hyatt* lists ways of making a meal together a good experience. Here are a few of his suggestions.

1. Ask open-ended questions, such as:

- What is your favorite music, best movie, etc., and why?

- What do you like most about (name a person in the family)?

- If running for President, what promise would you work hard to keep?

2. Involve everyone in the conversation: "What do you think?"

3. Do more listening than talking.

4. Affirm people, even if you disagree with them.

The point is to keep the conversation from focusing on negative ideas and criticism of people. Involve everyone and focus on a positive attitude to help make mealtime enjoyable.

Resource:
*michaelhyatt.com/how-to-have-better-dinner-conversations

Discussion Questions:
1. Describe the most relationally productive mealtimes you can remember.

2. What can each of you do to make eating together as a family at home more meaningful?

3. How can you make eating out a worthwhile family experience?

4. How can cell phones/technology devices be dealt with to encourage face-to-face communication during family meals?

Prayer Point/Take Away for Today:
At our next meal together, I will help keep the conversation going in a positive direction.

Notes/Responses/Action:

(Continued)

Notes/Responses/Action:

-35-

FOOD CULTURE

Read: Proverbs 31:14

Focus: Food comes from many sources.

Prior to the development of a well-organized delivery system, each area of the world had its own food culture, highly influenced by what was grown locally. When people from diverse food cultures met and married, there was often a strong contrast in food preferences and tastes. Merging a woman and a man from two radically different food cultures could have created an interesting and potentially challenging situation.

Even today, with the wide availability of foods from all over the world in one's local supermarket, there is still the potential of conflicting local food cultures. Each family has its own food culture. Food cultures vary from country to country and from family to family.

The possible contrasts range widely, even to the preferred store and down to the brand of peas.

Discussion Questions:

1. Take turns describing the food culture of your family of origin.

2. Think about when you first married. How did you handle the food differences each of you brought to your home? How easily did you merge your families' food cultures?

3. Describe the food culture of your present family situation.

4. What changes in foods would you like to try?

Prayer Point/Take Away for Today:
When new foods are introduced, I will participate and try to avoid complaining.

Notes/Responses/Action:

(Continued)

Notes/Responses/Action:

FOOD PREPARATION

Read: Genesis 1:29

Focus: There are many types of foods. Who prepares them?

With the huge availability of already prepared food, many persons grow up without significant kitchen skills. Rapidly paced living subsidizes supermarkets and fast food restaurants that require only a credit card to deliver a tempting meal to your home.

It is well documented that food prepared in restaurants is, by and large, less nutritious and less healthy than home-prepared meals. Eating out may be fun, but avoiding the kitchen can have long-term effects, both health-wise and in family bonding. Certainly, eating out on occasion can be helpful, especially when both spouses are worn out from work.

The important point here is to work together, with food preparation as an example. This may take a wide variety of forms. Some couples take turns or share food preparation responsibilities. Others designate one as the main chef while another has clean-up duty. Some specialize in shopping for food while the other prepares it. The possibilities are many, which include the ages of children in your family. Enjoy the pleasure of shared responsibilities related to food.

Discussion Questions:
1. What was it like in your home of origin concerning food shopping, preparation, serving, or clean up?

2. Describe your present food preparation culture. How are your children involved?

3. What changes might you want to discuss in terms of food preparation (broadly defined)?

Prayer Point/Take Away for Today:
I will be sensitive to my responsibility in food preparation.

Notes/Responses/Action:

(Continued)

Notes/Responses/Action:

-37-

EDUCATION

Read: Acts 7:22; Proverbs 23:12

Focus: Education can affect relationships.

In a world where education of large populations is a widespread goal, the diversity of academic backgrounds is very great. Even in recent generations, a college education was a rarity. With many persons attaining bachelor, master, and doctoral degrees, educational attainments for couples can vary widely.

It is not surprising that many couples meet while studying at similar educational levels. Because persons often become attracted to those they grew up near, however, some couples' backgrounds may range from high school graduates to graduate-level degrees. No matter the educational level differences, many more significant factors contribute toward a happy marriage.

Sometimes, the contrast in educational levels does show up in areas that require attention. For example, there may be large differences in musical appreciation, reading preferences, theatrical awareness, sports interests, and artistic tastes. How a couple deals with such contrasts can be critical.

Acceptance of dissimilarities is important. Working out how partners spend their free time based on educational backgrounds is significant. Neither partner should feel disenfranchised because of these differences. Don't let education negatively affect your relationship. Embrace the uniqueness of backgrounds that each of you brings to your marriage.

Discussion Questions:
1. Discuss your educational backgrounds, what or who influenced you educationally, and how you feel as a result of your education.

2. How do your educational experiences affect your perspective on leisure activities or other areas of your marriage?

3. If one or both of you want additional educational experiences, how might you go about achieving your goals?

Prayer Point/Take Away for Today:
I will relate to my spouse's educational background and goals in a positive manner.

Notes/Responses/Action:

(Continued)

Notes/Responses/Action:

LEISURE

Read: Exodus 33:14; Ephesians 5:15–16

Focus: Leisure is necessary but must be measured.

Regardless of how busy you are, there is always at least some free time — time not required by work, school, home, relatives, friends, or other commitments. The world has innumerable ways of occupying your free time. What are your favorite things to do when you are not required to be somewhere or do something?

You and your spouse each have preferences when there is nothing else to do. How well do these match?

A well-balanced couple should not be "joined at the hip". There should be both shared interests and separate interests. These can take many forms. The entertainment industry has created a diverse set of activities, many of which you can do together and many on your own.

1. TV, theater, and movies: What genre(s) do you prefer? How is the remote controlled?

2. Sports: Spectator? Participant? Both?

3. Games: Table, board games, cards, video/online games, etc.

4. Outdoor: Hiking, running, bird watching, flying, biking, nature photography, etc.

5. Collecting: Gathering objects of interest

6. Creativity and hobbies: Crafts, art, music, building, writing, repairing, remodeling, landscaping, inventing, experimenting, etc.

7. Reading: Which genre(s)?

Certain personality contrasts often result during the use of leisure time. Highly organized individuals may have specific times, places, and situations preset in the family calendar. On the other hand, spontaneous individuals are more prone to fast changes and decisions. These persons often marry each other. What conflicts might develop? How do you resolve leisure time conflicts? Hint: remember "give the gift of your opposition."

It is important for both of you to have fun in your leisure time. And it is also important to allocate some of your leisure time for service or church-related projects. More about this later.

Discussion Questions:
1. Discuss your preferred individual leisure time interests. How are they different or alike?

2. What do you like to do together during your leisure time?

3. How might you resolve differences in the ways you spend your leisure time?

Prayer Point/Take Away for Today:
When I have some leisure time, I will evaluate how I use it.

Notes/Responses/Action:

(Continued)

Notes/Responses/Action:

-39-

SERVICE

Read: Mark 12:30–31; Luke 10:25–37; Romans 12:6–8, 11;
2 Timothy 1:7; 1 Peter 4:10–11; Hebrews 6:10; James 2:24;
1 Corinthians 12:4

Focus: Christians are serving people.

From the earliest times of the church, Jesus' followers have been active in helping others. James instructs us that the two facets of the Christian life involve faith and works. He emphasized works as proof of faith (James 2:24). The church has sometimes vacillated between stressing faith or works. The facts of scripture clearly let us know that we are to develop both. Everyone, according to St. Paul, has been given gifts to use in helping others.

Too often, we make an excuse by listing what we can't do! A solution to this is to ask someone who knows us what our gifts are. Everyone has them. The parable of the Good Samaritan (Luke 10:25–37) provides a picture of why we do what we do. Christians are to be living examples of what Christ would do in our shoes. Humanity needs us to be Jesus for them. Nothing is more attractive to unbelievers than a Christian serving others. And nothing is a better excuse not to believe than a self-centered Christian who avoids using his/her gifts for God.

Discussion Questions:
1. Describe your God-given gifts of service. Be honest; this is not boasting. Be detailed.

2. What are some ways you have used your gifts, or how might you use your gifts?

3. What gifts are we each using or could be using in a ministry to others?

Prayer Points/Take Away for Today:
I will think of the best ways to use my God-given gifts.

Notes/Responses/Action:

(Continued)

Notes/Responses/Action:

TIME

Read: Ecclesiastes 3:1–8; Proverbs 16:9

Focus: Use time wisely.

Each person has an internal "clock" that goes off at various times. Some people like to be at events, such as church services, at least 15 minutes early. Others seem to be perpetually late or just squeak in the door on time.

Couples with these differences are often identified as having different organizational skills. Some are very organized and easily meet time obligations. Other individuals may be more spontaneous and act as the spirit moves. Of all the irritating contrasts found in couples, the use of time and possession of organizational skills may rank high on a regular basis. Some families develop helpful methods of dealing with tardy individuals' lack of ability to make appointments. Other families simply honk the horn to speed up those who move slower.

How a couple deals with their differences in managing time commitments is a topic to discuss. You can go online and find a myriad of examples dealing with how to increase your time management skills, but that is only part of the solution. Far better is to admit to each other that you have different internal clocks and decide how to adjust to your spouse's clock. Both of you may need to change some habits. Change in a couple's relationship usually involves a two-way street of behavior and attitude alterations.

Expect change to be a continuing part of your lives together. Believe it or not, change can energize your relationship.

Don't try to transform your spouse. That can be an exercise in futility. Lighten up and enjoy the journey.

Discussion Questions:
1. Describe your tendencies toward being late or overly punctual. Why do you think you are the way you are?

2. How has each of you adapted to your differences in dealing with time?

3. Are there any changes that you might consider making related to time?

4. Describe your organizational abilities and any contrasts you see.

5. How can you best use differences in your organizational skills to benefit your family?

Prayer Point/Take Away for Today:
I will evaluate my use of time.

Notes/Responses/Action:

(Continued)

Notes/Responses/Action:

-41-

ROLES

Read: Genesis 2:23–24; Ecclesiastes 4:9–12; Amos 3:3; Matthew 18:19

Focus: Be a dynamic duo!

In more traditional societal settings, there are expectations as to who will do what in the home. Today's society offers a wide range of options with gender often playing less of a role in doing tasks than in prior generations.

The same can be said for decision-making. You and/or your spouse may have come from family setting(s) where certain roles were understood or assigned. This is becoming less and less the norm.

There are a host of detailed tasks to be accomplished in a home. Think of the areas in your home where roles are necessary: food preparation, table clearing and dish washing, laundry, house cleaning, vehicle maintenance, lawn care, gardening, shopping, finances (discussed in the next devotional), and a host of others. If you have children, you also have their various needs to care for.

All these areas are important. There are no second-class responsibilities. How have you distributed your time and efforts in these areas? Do you treat some responsibilities with flexibility and others as sole responsibilities? Revisit your roles occasionally to adjust to the changing needs of your family.

Discussion Questions:

1. Describe roles in your families of origin. Where did you fit in?

2. How have you and your spouse decided to divide or share home responsibilities?

3. Should these responsibilities be re-evaluated and, if so, how?

4. What roles do you feel very uncomfortable doing?

5. What roles do you feel comfortable doing?

6. Where do your children fit in?

Prayer Point/Take Away for Today:
I will be open to changes in family roles.

Notes/Responses/Action:

(Continued)

Notes/Responses/Action:

-42-

DECISION-MAKING: MONEY

Read: Ecclesiastes 5:10; 1 Timothy 6:17–19; James 1:5

Focus: Develop a wise view of money.

Most of the decisions of life involve money, directly or indirectly. Even whether to have children or how many to have is a financial decision, considering the costs of raising a family. How you use your vacation time is an expense item. Health and exercise carry a price tag. Insurance of all types is not cheap. How do you supplement the benefits provided by your employer(s)? The list is endless and the choices to be made may seem never-ending. This is why you need to have continuing discussions involving decision-making in a wide variety of areas.

The process of deciding how to spend or use your resources can be a daunting task. Each of you comes from a different financial background where decisions were made in a variety of ways. How have you adapted to these differences? Some families spend most of their money as it becomes available. Others are tight-fisted and have serious controls on how money departs from their hands. For some, every want is a need, and for others, needs always precede wants. Some live with strict budgets and others live hand-to-mouth with all available funds spent early in the income-cycle.

Joining your different financial backgrounds may be one of the toughest parts of merging your lives in marriage. There are many ways of making financial decisions as a couple. It is important to be candid about your feelings concerning how you approach money and spending. Be open to discuss concerns each of you has about money and how it is used.

Most couples know that their view of money changes from when they were first married to the current time. Experience is a great teacher, although sometimes a harsh one. Learning to work as a team is critical, especially in the area of how money is spent.

Solving money problems together is essential for your family's financial health and well-being. Never be afraid to change if some financial approach is not working well. Be certain to seek God's wisdom in the decisions that you make.

Discussion Questions:
1. Describe how your family of origin made financial decisions. Where did you fit in?

2. Describe how you make financial decisions as a couple. Be specific.

3. What financial role do you feel very uncomfortable doing?

4. What financial role do you feel most comfortable doing?

5. What changes might be important to consider concerning how you deal with money?

Prayer Point/Take Away for Today:
I will rethink how I relate to family financial decision-making

Notes/Responses/Action:

-43-

FINANCES

Read: Proverbs 3:9–10, 13:11; Hebrews 13:5; Matthew 6:21; Malachi 3:10; 1 Chronicles 29:14

Focus: Be wise in spending, giving, and investing.

How you apply your financial skills in marriage is very important. Here is where the contrast between someone who is organized and someone who is spontaneous can wreak havoc in a marital relationship. How you settle this difference is no trivial matter.

Financial wisdom probably develops or comes to light early in life. Some are very skilled at handling money, while others spend freely, without much concern for the details. We all know individuals who are very adept with money and others who can't hold on to cash any better than they could hold a slippery fish. If these two types marry each other, this is a prescription for stress! Financial disaster awaits the family without a workable plan to which both can agree and follow.

Many couples use the default method of deciding who does what in terms of money. The person who is detail-oriented and is a planner often finds himself/herself handling the family finances. Under this scenario, one person is in charge of paying bills, saving for the future, allocating funds for various purposes, and keeping an eye on expenditures. This way, there is no uncertainty about how resources are used.

If the spouse less so endowed agrees with this approach, things can work out in this scenario. For this approach to work, however, the couple must have a clear understanding about and agree on making purchases. The caveats involved with this method are of concern. I know a person who gave every bit of the family finances to the spouse. When that spouse died, this person was totally frustrated, not knowing anything about the family finances: which banks, what investments, what property/mortgages, how to handle taxes, how to pay bills, etc. This was a catastrophe for that person.

To avoid such a disaster, it is very important to have as much full disclosure as possible. In other words, the bookkeeper shares with her/his spouse, at least monthly, as many details as possible. Have a checklist of important dates in the financial year and how these can be taken care of, in the case of incapacitation or death.

Both of you need to be on the same page, in terms of where you are financially and how you are proceeding toward agreed-upon goals. It also may help for the less-involved spouse to have some "mad money" to spend however she/he wishes, apart from family goals and plans. This may help keep a more spontaneous person from feeling left outside the financial situation.

Another approach some couples use is to divide the financial responsibilities. A host of options exist in this method. One spouse might be involved with routine bill paying and the other with discretionary spending. This requires very close communication so neither party overspends without the other's being aware and agreeing to changes.

Some couples keep separate accounts (his money and her money). This divided approach should involve continuous cross-checking to be certain that no area is out of balance.

Regardless of the approach, both parties must be aware of the expected responsibilities of each other. Periodic sharing of the details and expectations is key to a low-stress financial situation. Communication is vitally essential.

How money is spent is an issue for many marriages. Debt and differing views of borrowing can be a big problem. Going into debt should be discussed thoroughly before signing the loan commitment form.

Today's financial world is a complicated place. Each spouse should learn as much as possible so they are working toward common goals and planning effectively for the future: careers, children, retirement, etc. Learn together about how to manage money. There are many useful websites and books on how to deal with finances. Money may not seem to be a romantic subject, but romance can evaporate quickly when the financial wheels fall off the relationship.

There are a host of models* to use in deciding how to spend money, but one thing should be common throughout the marital relationship of Christians: all resources are ultimately gifts from God. Appropriate return of funds for His purposes (the tithe) has remained throughout the history of Judaism and Christianity. Those who practice faithful giving often testify to the blessing of God on their lives and resources.

Resources: (**Note:** They do not agree on some points!)
*https://www.forbes.com/sites/jenniferwoods/2015/07/06/10-ways-to-prevent-money-from-ruining-your-marriage/#1d208e9e44c9
*https://www.daveramsey.com/blog/the-truth-about-money-and-relationships
*https://www.usatoday.com/story/money/personalfinance/2017/07/05/pros-and-cons-sharing-your-finances-married-couple/438157001/

Discussion Questions:

1. Describe your background in terms of your philosophy of money, i.e., how you view money, how financial decisions were made in your family of origin, what you fear about financial decisions, etc.

2. How would you describe your present approach, as a couple, to your family's finances?

3. Describe your comfort level concerning giving back to God.

4. What changes might you consider important as you look forward to your family's financial future?

Prayer Point/Take Away for Today:
I will rethink my philosophy of money.

Notes/Responses/Action:

(Continued)

Notes/Responses/Action:

CONTROLLING MONEY

Read: Deuteronomy 8:18a; Proverbs 11:24; Matthew 7:12

Focus: God gives us the ability to have wealth. Be generous.

Say the word "budget," and everyone cringes. The human mind tends to snag on a restrictive picture of spending that takes all the fun out of living. Contrary to popular disinterest in or fear of budgeting, there does not have to be agony associated with controlled spending.

Why do we have to talk about budgets? The reason is simple: money is at the heart of too much of what we do in our lives. We will either control money or money will control us. Chaos reigns if income is less than expenditures. The only way to avoid this is to work together for achieving agreed-on goals and tackling the tough financial decisions.

A way to begin controlling money involves adding up the fixed expenses that you know and subtracting these from your take-home cash. Estimate your flexible expenses (those things that are variable, like food, clothing, entertainment, etc.) and subtract them from the remaining income. If the remainder is positive, pat yourself on the back. If negative, then flexible expenses need your attention.

This requires serious work by both of you. Always include a line item that has no purpose other than how each of you wants to spend it (*mad money*). Whatever method you decide to use to keep track of your income/expenses, both of you must be involved in basic decisions. Both must know what is going on and have a significant say in the decisions.*

Resources: (Note: They do not agree on some points!)
*https://www.forbes.com/sites/jenniferwoods/2015/07/06/10-ways-to-prevent-money-from-ruining-your-marriage/#1d208e9e44c9
*https://www.daveramsey.com/blog/the-truth-about-money-and-relationships
*https://www.usatoday.com/story/money/personalfinance/2017/07/05/pros-and-cons-sharing-your-finances-married-couple/438157001/

Discussion Questions:
1. Describe your thoughts about how to control expenses as they relate to income. Have you tried a budget of some sort? If so, how did (does) it work for you? Should you consider changes?

2. How might your involvement in controlling expenses be helpful for you to reach your goals?

3. Describe your thoughts about using a budget (if you are not using one) as a method of financial control.

Prayer Point/Take Away for Today:
I will evaluate our family's approach to spending and controlling our money.

Notes/Responses/Action:

(Continued)

Notes/Responses/Action:

-45-

STAYING IN LOVE

Read: Ephesians 4:2–3; Galatians 6:10

Focus: Be consistently in love.

Relationships do not run on air. You must continually nourish each other and feed love vitamins. You have probably seen your fair share of TV/movie/theater examples of how a marriage can grind to a halt. The reasons are many: poor money management, lack of attention to each other, a boring lifestyle, unsatisfied sexual needs, outside distractions, family issues, health concerns, and a host of other problems.

Someone described the attention of a man pursuing a woman as a marriage partner in this way. He is running after a moving bus, exerting a lot of effort. Once he jumps on the bus, he sits down in a seat, breathes a sigh of relief, and relaxes. The rest of marriage is a dull ride on the bus! He has caught his ride, so what else is there to do?

On the other side, a woman may do quite a bit to be alluring until she lands him. Then she may relax and go about life in a routine manner, letting her appearance deteriorate. Too often these two models match many marriages. Each spouse has nothing more to do after the match has been made.

Studies of successful marriages do not agree with this dreary tedium. Spouses who are continually attentive to each other and their needs almost universally maintain love at a level that

144

keeps the love vitamins flowing! A huge diversity exists within successful marriages in terms of details, but many features show up again and again. Successful couples almost never take each other for granted. They generally maintain a sense of attraction for each other with ways that the spouse understands as his/her love language. Refer back to the five love languages for keeping the spark alive and well-maintained.

Domination by one or the other spouse rarely shows up in happy marriages; equality is normal. The spouses tend to share responsibilities and decision-making. Age seems to have little impact on happy marriages. After interviewing happy couples married for 60, 70, or more years, we found a growth of mature love that kept them attuned to each other.

The statistics of divorce can be discouraging but are often misquoted.* Divorce rates have fallen for many years. The often misquoted 40 to 50 percent divorce rate is questionable. The actual number is apparently lower than this range. Second and third marriages often fair worse than first marriages, but the quoted statistics also appear to be significantly inflated. If statistics tend to frighten you, here is a truth: *statistics only work for groups, not on an individual basis.* You decide (remember the gift of free choice God gives you) *not* to become a divorce statistic!

Happiness is essentially a decision you make. Agree together to be successful. Focus on making your spouse happy and fulfilled.

Resource:
The Good News About Marriage, Shaunti Feldhahn,
WaterBrook Multnomah books.

Discussion Questions:
1. What drew us together in the first place?

2. What can we do to enhance our love relationship?

3. How can we continue to grow our marriage?

4. How might we deal with an illiness that strikes one of us, our children, or our parents?

Prayer Point/Take Away for Today:
I will do something today to enhance our love relationship.

Notes/Responses/Action:

(Continued)

Notes/Responses/Action:

-46-

TOGETHERNESS

Read: Ecclesiastes 4:9–10; Romans 12:3–5

Focus: Couples are to be one "body."

Happy marriages involve couples who enjoy being together. This is not the hip-joined problem some couples display. As a couple, you also need to have connections with friends and organizations outside the home, but these must not distract from your primary connectivity with each other.

Plan times to be together, without distractions. If money is tight and children are involved, this may require careful planning and creativity. Couples sometimes share child care with other couples while they have special times by themselves. And it is possible to arrange togetherness without leaving home. This requires saving enough energy and time to withdraw to a spot where you can focus on each other, stare into each other's eyes, and share dreams and ideas. Spending money is not a necessity to grow your relationship. The decision to be together with minimum distractions is a key component.

Find places to be together. This might be an inexpensive café or a park bench. Setting aside money for a shared vacation is also a great idea. The busyness of life can sap your energy and leave little time to share, dream, and say how much you care for each other.

Married sex often finds maximum fulfillment after this time of togetherness. Don't assume that sex is your only "togetherness" time. Meaningful kitchen-talk can be a great prelude to sexual intimacy, and so can shared prayer. Time is the most important commodity you have, and the wise use of this resource together is fundamental for a strong relationship.

Discussion Questions:
1. How do we spend time together? Are we spending time in meaningful talk?

2. How might we use shared time to enhance our relationship?

3. Life can be hectic. How do we find time for us as a couple?

Prayer Point/Take Away for Today:
I will take time to sit down and talk with my spouse.

Notes/Responses/Action:

(Continued)

Notes/Responses/Action:

-47-

SEX AND ALL THAT STUFF!

Read: Hebrews 13:4; Proverbs 5:18–20; 1 Corinthians 7:3–5

Focus: Enjoy marital sex!

Our society is, to say the least, sex-saturated. Check the list of current movies for their ratings: R often dominates, with explicit sex between unmarried couples frequently portrayed. The undergirding premise is the hedonistic view that sex is simply biological pleasure. No wonder that marital sex is portrayed as inferior to extramarital affairs and one-night stands with some hot person.

This sad state portrays sex as something that is done just for fun with no strings attached. God never intended this distortion of His wonderful creation.

St. Paul lived in a sex-dominated society too. Prostitution occurred in pagan temple worship. Sex was literally part of some groups' religion! Paul sounded a clear alarm and referred back to the original plan of God that sex is for committed marriage because of the intimate nature of the relationship. The oneness that is biologically and psychologically built into sexual love is unique among humans, compared to simple copulation in the rest of the organic world. The media portray sex as just a casual thing that is no more than personal physical satisfaction. This is the antithesis of Christian marriage.

Modern Western society tends to deify love as an all-consuming purpose. It should be no surprise that those living in the fast lane lose out on the beauty of marital love that is grounded in a lifelong commitment. To expect continuous emotional highs just because copulation occurs has led to innumerable relationship disasters built on this flimsy foundation.

Successful sexual expressions in marriage will never provide long-term satisfaction if physical stimulation is the only outcome. Happy, lasting marriages embody a unity that comes from joining all facets of the relationship: physical, emotional, spiritual, intellectual, and social. Meeting the love language needs of each other is basic for a satisfying sexual love life together.

Of course, sexual intimacy requires awareness of the physical needs of each other. Honest discussion of what each prefers during intimate times is important. Being open can resolve hidden concerns that might otherwise go unspoken. And don't be afraid to refer to some of the excellent Christian books on sexual techniques.*

Resource:
The Gift of Sex, Clifford and Joyce Penner, Word Publishing.

Discussion Questions:
1. Describe your perspective on sexual intimacy.

2. How might our sexual expressions to each other be used to strengthen our relationship?

3. What could we do to enhance our sexual intimacy?

Prayer Point/Take Away for Today:
I will be more in tune with my spouse's sexual needs.

Notes/Responses/Action:

-48-

ROMANTIC MYTH

Read: Proverbs 4:23–27

Focus: Reserve romance for your spouse.

The idea of choosing a marriage partner for romantic reasons dates from only the 18th century in Western societies. Arranged marriages were common before then. People learned to love each other after marriage.

Romance now dominates much of the material in books, movies, and theatrical performances. But what does it take to remain romantic after the "I do"? Contrary to popular myths, the need for a ravishing, curvy female and a tall, suave male to have romance is fictitious. Romance is a state of mind. What one person deems romantic is not the same for all individuals. Just as everyone has a primary love language, secondary love language, etc., so everyone has their own perspective on what is romantic.

One person may think a candlelight dinner with crystal glasses and fine china is essential for a romantic evening.* The other spouse may consider such trappings as a boring prelude to the real stuff in bed! You can come close to guessing what your spouse sees as romantic by going back to his/her love language. There isn't a direct correlation, but how he/she understands love may be partly related to how he/she understands romance!

Romantic feelings are just that: emotions. So, ask yourself what turns on your spouse's emotions in a positive way. Don't force your concept of romance onto your spouse. It might be that the best thing to do is talk about how each of you sees romance. This may seem way too analytical, but otherwise you may nibble around the edge of romance without really experiencing its full emotional flare! Talk about romance with each other. You might be surprised by what you learn!

Resources:
*A fun book that you might want to explore is *1001 Ways to be Romantic*, Gregory J.P. Godek, Casablanca Press.
*A book which explores how to reverse a marriage headed the wrong way is *Divorce Busting*, Michele Weiner-Davis, Fireside, and Simon and Schuster.
*An example book on keeping love alive is *2002 Ways to Say "I Love You"*, Cyndi Haynes and Dale Edwards, Adams Media Corporation.

Discussion Questions:
1. Describe your concept of romance.

2. How might we use romance to enhance our relationship?

Prayer Point/Take Away for Today:
I will think of ways to enhance our romance.

(Continued)

Notes/Responses/Action:

-49-

WHAT IS LOVE?

Read: Ephesians 5:21–33; 1 Corinthians 13

Focus: Love covers a lot of territory.

You know the soppy, dewy-eyed view of love portrayed on TV, in movies, and in romance novels. It is the idea that you will automatically know that "this is the one" by some mysterious feeling. This is amazingly pervasive in American society.

But what happens when the rose-colored glasses are removed and your stomach doesn't have the quivers anymore? Do you "fall out of love" just as quickly as you "fell in love"? Or how about the all-too-common excuse: "I don't love you anymore"? These all reflect a view that love is a "feeling" that you will know and recognize automatically.

So, what about the couple who has all the right feelings and, after marriage, their feelings go down the tube? Must they live a wretched existence without those wonderful sensations they knew before? Is there more to love than having the right vibrations?

Let's look at the kinds of love in the Greek language and found in the New Testament.*

1. *Eros*: Erotic love associated with male-female attraction and related to sex.

2. *Philia*: Friendship love, used when referring to those with whom we have close communication and share our inner thoughts.

3. *Storge*: Family love, not used in the New Testament but refers to the bonds that hold families together.

4. *Agape*: Divine love or Christian love, such as described in 1 Corinthians 13. This is selfless love that looks out for the best in someone else.

In Ephesians 5:25, St. Paul says that husbands are to show this sacrificial Christian love (*agape*) to their wives. In the culture of Paul's day, wives were already expected to do this. So Paul brings wives and husbands to the same level by requiring husbands to be *agape* lovers! In Ephesians 5:21, Paul casts an umbrella over the succeeding verses, which are often misunderstood in our culture and misused to suggest dominance and have led to abuse.**

Agape love is the goal for Christian couples. How different 1 Corinthians 13 is from the strictly erotic love foisted onto Americans by the media. Certainly there is erotic love in a Christian marriage, but *agape* love doesn't depend on feelings. Instead, *agape* love is based on care and commitment! Erotic love may draw you together, but *agape* love transforms your relationship into a beautiful bond that the pagan world knows nothing about. Go for the *agape*!

Resources:
Easy to Live With, Leslie Parrott, Beacon Hill Press, Kansas City.
**https://www.focusonthefamily.com/family-q-and-a/relationships-and-marriage/submission-of-wives-to-husbands

Discussion Questions:
1. Read 1 Corinthians 13 aloud together and discuss the implications of *agape* love in your relationship.

2. What can we do to increase any of the other loves in our relationship, e.g., *philia* love and *storge* love?

Prayer Point/Take Away for Today:
I will think of some new ways to show *agape* love to my spouse.

Notes/Responses/Action:

(Continued)

Notes/Responses/Action:

-50-

CRITICISM

Read: Proverbs 14:29; Romans 12:19

Focus: Keep a lid on critical talk.

TV family humor often centers on criticism of various members of the family. This may be funny, but where does criticism fit into your family? Criticism is typically focused on someone's weaknesses, which we all have. Nobody is without flaws, and some are quite glaring. Do we know that we have flaws? Most of us are quite aware of our own weaknesses and failures. We don't really have to be told about them to make us aware of their existence. Criticism is essentially a negative experience.

Negative experiences dominate our lives in the real world. We really do not need to have our loved ones pour more negativity on us. What do we need? The research tells us that positives are what we need to counter the negative influences.* This is not the same thing as the "everybody wins" stuff in some areas of sports. The truth is that we need to put the *emphasis* on what we do right, not on our known-to-us weaknesses.

A couple who communicates effectively has learned that approaching a problem by helping lift the burden, rather than increasing the weight, is best. When approaching a sensitive issue, use the magic "I" word to remove the antagonistic "you" word from talks. When describing how a behavior makes you feel, the onus shifts to a discussion of what can help, instead of raising resentment over the attack of a sore spot. "I feel ill at ease when I sense that you are angry with me for ___" is far better than "You always get angry when ___."

The idea is not to ignore a problem, but to approach it in a non-threatening way, if possible. When tempted to be critical, pause and think what the reaction of your spouse may be when hearing your snide comment. Easy does it. Leave criticism to the sit-coms!

Resource:
Why Marriages Succeed or Fail, John Gottman, Fireside, Simon and Schuster.

Discussion Questions:
1. How does being critical make you feel? How does being criticized make you feel?

2. This week, how can we avoid making critical comments?

3. How can we practice using "I" statements to express issues we have with each other?

Prayer Point/Take Away for Today:
I will use "I" statements instead of "you" statements when things get tense between my spouse and me.

Notes/Responses/Action:

(Continued)

Notes/Responses/Action:

-51-

SAY WHAT'S IMPORTANT

Read: Galatians 6:2; 1 Peter 1:22

Focus: Carry one another's burdens.

How do you say what is important in your marital relationship? Instead of being ambiguous, state it clearly. For example, a wonderful conversation might begin with: "I want you to know how important our relationship is to me." Then go on to describe what this marriage relationship means to you. You might share your vision of how you would like to improve your connection with your spouse. This can keep your conversations from becoming boring or repetitious. Each of us sees things differently, so share your vision and lift your discussion to a new level. Say what is important to you. Build on your strengths.*

Philip Yancey shares this about his marriage: "... the very differences ... personality, outlook, and daily routine — actually represent a great strength. Janet provides me with a new set of eyes into a world I barely know about ... I marvel at the differences in temperament and spiritual gifts that allow her to spend her day dealing with situations that would probably drive me crazy."**

Resources:
Empowering Couples, 2nd edition, David H. Olson and Amy K. Olson, Life Innovations, Inc.
**Grace Notes*, Philip Yancey, Zondervan.

Discussion Questions:

1. What topics about our relationship could we discuss that we haven't touched on before?

2. How can we increase the level of our conversations?

Prayer Point/Take Away for Today:

I will do my best to say some things that are important to me, but I will say them gently and with grace.

Notes/Responses/Action:

(Continued)

Notes/Responses/Action:

-52-

THE "MAGIC QUESTION"

Read: Proverbs 31:10–11; Ephesians 5:25

Focus: Be respectful and sacrificial toward each other.

Let's say that you sense something is bothering your spouse. How do you approach him/her to help? There are many things you could say to assist the discussion. Here is one that is almost universally applicable and least invasive: **"What do you need from me right now?"**

This can often loosen the logjam of feelings bottled up within her/him. Perhaps she/he can then open up and reveal what is bothering her/him.

Be prepared to empathize as best you can. Silence may be more important in some circumstances. Just listen carefully. Don't try to heal or repair. Your spouse may tell you what the needs are. If not, don't despair. Quietness may be most important at this specific time. Give the gift of persistent silence as needed.

Discussion Questions:

1. How might the "magic question" help?

2. When might we have used this in our relationship?

3. How could the "magic question" be important to us as a couple?

Notes/Responses/Action:

-53-

FAMILY ISSUES: TRADITIONS

Read: Psalm 68:6a; 1 Timothy 5:8

Focus: Family traditions are important.

There is strong agreement among those who work with couples that you do indeed marry a family. You cannot escape your backgrounds. You can choose which parts of your background to keep and what you don't want to bring into your marital relationship. Yet, the past colors your life, one way or another.

Don't despair over this. Learn to use past family backgrounds as a backdrop for making decisions in your family. Keep the good. Refuse to include the bad.

Differences between families can be huge. This shows up in a couple's household chores, food preferences, entertainment, hygiene, and many other areas. Family traditions involving holidays often create tensions until you, as a couple, decide how to deal with them in a way that works out best.

Holiday traditions can be deeply embedded in a family's culture. Think about how you have worked through the decisions about who to visit, when, and how long to stay. There is an old adage that relatives who stay longer than three days are a bit like fish left out for three days! Don't take this literally, but be aware of when it is time to leave!

You, as a couple, have your own culture. It is important to build on the strengths each of you brings to the relationship.*

Resource:
**Empowering Couples*, 2nd edition, David H. Olson and Amy K. Olson, Life Innovations, Inc.

Discussion Questions:
1. Take turns describing your family of origin's holiday traditions. What part did you play in those traditions? How meaningful were those traditions to you?

2. How have we resolved differences of holiday traditions between our families of origin?

3. How have we developed our own family traditions, and how satisfied are we with them? Do we need to re-evaluate some things?

Prayer Point/Take Away for Today:
I will think about any holiday traditions that we need to discuss.

Notes/Responses/Action:

(Continued)

Notes/Responses/Action:

-54-

FAMILY ISSUES: CHILDREN AND PARENTING

Read: Psalm 127:3; Proverbs 22:6; Matthew 19:13–15; Ephesians 6:1–2

Focus: Parenting is a big responsibility.

Having children is a big decision and not to be treated casually. Theoretically, most anyone can biologically produce children. But to be a person who takes parenting seriously requires much more than biology! Effective parenting involves time and energy in huge doses. If you have children, a principle to remember is this: **Children need abundant amounts of your time and energy at *all stages* of their lives.**

Here is a caveat: **You never outgrow being a parent!** From infant to adult, they are always your children. This doesn't mean that you treat them as small children all their lives! You and your children pass through many phases. You will nurse, train, discipline, guide, release, and encourage independence.

There is no magic formula to follow (think of all the parenting books!) It is, however, fundamentally important to provide a model for living that your children can observe and find reasonably attractive, at least in later years! You are "normal" for your children. That is a sobering thought as you live your life before them.

Since children move through many stages during their lives, it is imperative that you and your spouse change and adapt to their stages as well. You can't treat a teenager like a fourth grader. Be nimble on your parental feet! Children can change rapidly. Effective parenting requires you to change your parenting approach in tune with each child's stage and characteristics.*

No two children are exactly the same. Personalities can be quite different, and their response to your parenting skills will likely not be the same. Treat each child as a unique individual. In case you haven't noticed, parenting is not for wimps!

Resource:
Different Children, Different Needs, The Art of Adjustable Parenting, Charles F. Boyd, Multnomah Books.

Discussion Questions:
1. Describe your relationship with your parents. How did they change their parenting styles as you matured?

2. Evaluate changes we have each made as parents as our children have grown (assuming we have children).

3. Are there changes to discuss relative to our current parenting styles?

Prayer Point/Take Away for Today:
I will be conscious of how to behave as a parent, relative to the maturity of our children.

Notes/Responses/Action:

-55-

FAMILY ISSUES: CHILDREN AND DISCIPLINE

Read: Ephesians 6:4; Colossians 3:21; Leviticus 19:32

Focus: Disciplining children requires care.

Think about your family of origin and how your parents disciplined you. Did their approach to discipline change as you matured? Do you wish your parents had behaved toward you in a different manner, in terms of discipline?

How has your experience growing up in your family of origin impacted your own perspective of discipline? If you have children, how have you decided, as a couple, to handle discipline?

Abuse of any kind has no place in parenting. Neither is permissive, total freedom appropriate in disciplining children. A rigid approach that treats each child exactly alike ignores the uniqueness inherent in children. Each child has her/his own personality, which you should honor and respect. Discipline should reflect the child's personality and how the child responds to your approach.

There is no universal solution to a child's resistance to discipline! Treat each child according to what works best for him/her. No two children are alike; relate to them in ways that honor their uniquenesses.*

Pay attention to your child's maturing phases. Ignoring their changes can be disastrous. Keep alert to your child's questions and tendencies. They give clues to how you may need to modify your parenting approach.

Resource:
Different Children, Different Needs, The Art of Adjustable Parenting, Charles F. Boyd, Multnomah Books.

Discussion Questions:
1. Describe how your parents disciplined you. Were their methods effective? If not, what should they have done differently?

2. Describe our concepts of discipline for children (whether or not we have children).

3. Are there changes to disciplining our children that we might consider?

Prayer Point/Take Away for Today:
I will evaluate how I discipline our children.

Notes/Responses/Action:

(Continued)

Notes/Responses/Action:

-56-

FAMILY ISSUES: CHILDREN AND SPIRITUALITY

Read: Deuteronomy 4:9, 6:4–7; Matthew 19:14

Focus: Bring your children to Jesus.

The early Hebrews were very direct in the religious training of their children. They were to talk and live out their religious beliefs as examples of how their children should grow up to be followers of God.

In Jesus' youth, He followed the precepts taught in his home and formal houses of worship.

Timothy was taught by his mother and apparently by his grandmother. These teachings resulted in Timothy's becoming a wonderful New Testament Christian (1 Timothy 1:5).

How can we apply these biblical examples in our homes today? Each culture and generation must learn how to become followers of Jesus Christ in ways that will impact the world in which they live.

Spiritual training begins early. The idea of leaving spirituality up to the child is never illustrated in the Bible. The home has always been central for spiritual training. Formal worship and church school provide group experiences and helpful methods for spiritual growth, but it is in the Christian home where the main training should take place.

Discussion Questions:

1. What was the spiritual atmosphere in your home of origin?

2. How did you react to concepts you learned about God, church, salvation, etc. in your home?

3. How does your religious upbringing impact your life today?

4. Describe how your spiritual background might have an impact on our present home?

5. At the stages where our children are (if we have children), what changes are they passing through? What are our responsibilities in assisting their spiritual growth?

Prayer Point/Take Away for Today:

I will re-evaluate how I relate to our children spiritually.

Notes/Responses/Action:

(Continued)

Notes/Responses/Action:

-57-

GOALS

Read: Romans 8:28; Philippians 3:12–14

Focus: Never stop moving forward.

Everyone has goals or directions he/she wants his/her life to take. When you and your spouse were dating, you no doubt discussed goals and plans. Goals are important because they tend to shape our focus and direction in life.

Financial planners suggest an annual review of investments. Another wise process is to review your personal and family goals annually. Nobody's goal is unimportant. All may not carry equal weight, but all should be heard and discussed.

There needs to be lots of give and take in discussions of goals. Take your time; this is not necessarily a quick process. It certainly is not an easy process either. Cover the discussions with prayer. Allow God's Spirit to guide you. Enjoy the excitement of mutual goal setting! And revisit your goals often. They will likely continue to change as time progresses.

Melding the various sets of personal, couple, and family goals is not a trivial task. Involve everyone in the family, once children are old enough to understand what is going on. They have goals, too!

Discussion Questions:
1. Reflect back on the goals you had as individuals and as a couple before you were married. How have your goals changed since you married?

2. Are there goals of an earlier time that you would like to revisit and consider now or in the future?

3. Each make a list of current individual, couple, and family goals. Compare lists. How alike or unlike are our goals?

4. Are our present goals exciting? What will it take to accomplish these goals? How will we establish priority in accomplishing our goals?

Prayer Point/Take Away for Today:
I will re-evaluate my goals in relation to my spouse's goals and our family goals.

Notes/Responses/Action:

(Continued)

Notes/Responses/Action:

(Continued)

Notes/Responses/Action:

58

EXPECTATIONS

Read: Joshua 1:9; Romans 5:3–5; 1 Peter 5:7

Focus: Let God guide your future.

Everyone entering marriage has expectations. No one anticipates an unhappy marriage. No one thinks there will a disastrous divorce. Most are wearing slightly rose-tinted glasses. And that is how it should be. If a couple was harmed by divorce, then something happened between "I do" and "I'm out of here!"

There are plenty of studies trying to tease out what slams the door on *happy* and admits *sadness* into a marriage relationship. Fortunately, although marriage requires work, it is not rocket science! Probably the most important thing is to look first at what makes happy marriages work.

One of the top items for happiness in marriage is **how a couple communicates with each other.*** This involves being open and honest, while maintaining full respect, and includes looking level-eyed at each other (i.e., seeing each other as equals with nobody in this relationship below the other).

Hot on the heels of this is the need for an abundance of positive feelings expressed to each other, along with a willingness to apologize for mistakes. We could stop there because such an approach leaves petty differences and selfishness in the dust.

There are lots of other characteristics, which we have explored in prior devotionals, but learning to communicate with the opposite gender in an atmosphere of love and acceptance will trump almost everything else. Getting to this level of communication is not easy, since we all have baggage that can shortcut our higher goals.

The main point: A married couple can usually resolve other issues if they strive for a deep level of communication saturated with respect, positive feelings, and apologies. Then you are moving toward meeting your anticipated expectations!

Resource:
The Relationship Cure, John M. Gottman and Joan DeClaire, Crown Publishers.

Discussion Questions:
1. What are our expectations going forward in our marriage?

2. How can our expectations grow our relationship?

3. What do we need from each other to meet our expectations?

Prayer Point/Take Away for Today:
I will take time to re-evaluate my expectations and improve my communication with my spouse.

Notes/Responses/Action:

(Continued)

Notes/Responses/Action:

59

GROWING, COACHING, AND COUNSELING

Read: Proverbs 8:14, 15:22

Focus: Seek help when needed.

All couples need to continue growing their relationship. Many churches and parachurch groups offer weekend retreats, classes, or other venues designed to help couples build their relationships. See your local church or organization about these services.

When a couple feels stuck and wants to move forward, but hasn't been successful in finding ways to overcome getting past being stuck, it might be time to consider coaching or counseling.

Life coaches assist couples in processing their dreams and help them discover ways to move forward toward their goals.

Counselors typically work with couples to discern what may be the root issues for being stuck, or why they are unable to communicate or resolve problems. This may allow the couple to begin making progress together.

Many organizations, educational institutions, and churches offer counseling resources. If you feel that you would profit from such help, contact your pastor, local coaching or counseling agency, educational resource, etc. about providing these services.

Professional counselors and life coaches will typically charge per session. Pastors may or may not charge. Most sessions typically last from a half-hour to an hour. There is no uniform number of sessions that you can expect.

The willingness of you and your spouse to make appropriate changes is key to making coaching or counseling work. Look at these experiences not as scary, but as opportunities to grow.

Discussion Question:
If appropriate, discuss seeking assistance to build your marriage.

Prayer Point/Take Away for Today:
I will think about ways to build our marriage.

Notes/Responses/Action:

-60-

WRAPPING IT UP

Read: Ecclesiastes 7:8–9

Focus: Go on from here.

"It is easier to start than to finish" (a quote from Carol, my wife). Almost anyone can get married. But to have a happy, successful marriage requires effort and a willingness to do the work in a spirit of love and acceptance.

Fortunately, you don't have to go it alone! God, the Creator of the universe and you, wants the best for both of you. He will stick with you in the ups and downs of life. Jesus Christ died to provide you with salvation and a heavenly home. Plus, He gives the Holy Spirit to energize you and sustain you throughout life.

The bottom line: Be the best soulmates you can be!

As you have worked through the questions in this book, hopefully you have discovered more about each other and more about the God who made you. To continue to grow, continue to share devotions with each other by using one of the many helpful books and guides available. I wish you God's best in the process of growing your marriage.

Finally, consider the relationship ladder. Imagine a ladder from the side. You are at one leg, and your spouse is at the other leg. At the top of the ladder is God. Imagine steps on both legs of the ladder. As each of you climbs the ladder, two things happen. You individually come closer to God, and you come closer to each other.

Strive to be all that God has in store for you, and move forward in a beautiful unity with each other. God wants the best for you. Communicate with Him and with each other. That is an unbeatable combination!

Discussion Questions:

1. Review what stands out as you think back over your discussions using this book.
2. Talk about how you want to proceed from here.

Prayer Point/Take Away for Today:
Thank God for my spouse!

Notes/Responses/Action:

(Continued)

Notes/Responses/Action:

(Continued)

Notes/Responses/Action:

MY PRAYER FOR YOU

Jesus, please give this couple a sense of your presence each day of their lives. May they seek your will and depend on your grace to guide them in the decisions they make as partners through life. Help them to see the great potential in their family to bring about your Kingdom on Earth. May love be their underlying principle in all their conversations. Give your guiding Spirit to them so that divine wisdom is evident in how they lead their family. May their shared faith be the source of their love. Help their family to be an example of what you want for all people.

In your great Name, Amen

ABOUT THE AUTHOR

Max W. Reams, B.A., B.S., M.S., M.P.C. (Master of Pastoral Counseling), Ph.D., LL.D. (honorary) is married to Carol A. (Cushard) Reams, A.A., B.S., M.P.C. They have three children, five grandchildren, and great-grandchildren, too. He taught 50 years at Olivet Nazarene University. He is a Trainer for Life Innovation, Inc. (Prepare-Enrich premarital/marital assessment). He is a Certified Life Coach. He and Carol are Volunteer Chaplains. They have led numerous retreats for married couples and worked with many premarital and married couples.

Made in the USA
Lexington, KY
17 October 2019